Be the Dog

Be the Dog

SECRETS OF THE NATURAL DOG OWNER

Steve Duno

STERLING

New York / London
www.sterlingpublishing.com

STERLING and the distinctive Sterling logo are registered trademarks of
Sterling Publishing Co., Inc.

Library of Congress Cataloging-in-Publication Data

Duno, Steve.
  Be the dog : secrets of the natural dog owner / Steve Duno.
    p. cm.
  Includes index.
  ISBN-13: 978-1-4027-2283-7
  ISBN-10: 1-4027-2283-4
  1. Dog owners—Psychology. 2. Dogs—Psychological aspects.
  3. Human-animal relationships. I. Title.

SF422.86.D86 2008
636.7'0887—dc22
                        2007027697

10 9 8 7 6 5 4 3 2 1

Published by Sterling Publishing Co., Inc.
387 Park Avenue South, New York, NY 10016
© 2008 by Steve Duno
Distributed in Canada by Sterling Publishing
C/o Canadian Manda Group, 165 Dufferin Street
Toronto, Ontario, Canada M6K 3H6
Distributed in the United Kingdom by GMC Distribution Services
Castle Place, 166 High Street, Lewes, East Sussex, England BN7 1XU
Distributed in Australia by Capricorn Link (Australia) Pty. Ltd.
P.O. Box 704, Windsor, NSW 2756, Australia

Sterling ISBN-13: 978-1-4027-2283-7
        ISBN-10: 1-4027-2283-4

For information about custom editions, special sales, premium and
corporate purchases, please contact Sterling Special Sales
Department at 800-805-5489 or specialsales@sterlingpublishing.com.

Contents

PART ONE

Forgotten Connections:
The Changing Dog/Owner Dynamic

In the mid-nineteenth century, gold rush fever lured the world's hopefuls to the American West. Among those who came were the Basques, people from an obscure mountainous region straddling the border of France and Spain. Already established in South America and Australia, they would now try their luck here.

Though some Basques did find their fortunes in gold, many more came to embrace a different destiny, one inextricably entwined with two other iconic characters: the merino sheep and the herding dog.

The sheer numbers of those drawn to America's Golden West spawned other industries, among them ranching and sheepherding, needed to feed and clothe the westward pioneers. Sensing opportunity, Basques offered their services as sheepherders to shrewd businessmen bringing stock out West. With the Basques came the collies, English Shepherds and other Sheepdogs of the day, archetypes of modern herding breeds such as the Australian Shepherd, Border and Bearded Collies, and others.

These were serious dogs. The climate and terrain of the American West demanded it, as did the millions of sheep shipped into California's ports. Unlike in Europe or South America, where herds rarely topped a thousand, American sheep herds often numbered ten times that. Developed in Spain, the merino sheep produced a fine-grade wool, and were noted for their hardiness and strong herding instincts, making them a good choice for the harsh conditions found in the American West.

Dogs in charge of managing such mammoth herds had to be hardy, smart, and independent-minded. The Basques depended on their dogs to move the huge flocks far and wide in search of fresh grazing land.

The dogs spent cold days alone with their sheep, watching, worrying, outsmarting, and making up rules as they went along. They had purpose, heart, and resolve, and were doing what herders had been asked to do for five thousand years. It was a birthright they felt in their hearts and bones and, when they finally curled up to sleep at night, they dreamed of stray lambs and willful rams, and whimpered and ran in their sleep. They had purpose, and they knew it.

Few dogs live that kind of austere, purpose-driven life anymore. We wouldn't want them to, as it was in retrospect a brutal, dangerous world, one in which the dog/owner relationship was utilitarian at best. But back then, they and the Basques needed each other. There was affection, to be sure; but first and foremost was an understanding of the job at hand, and a mutual respect for the other's abilities. There existed a natural, unspoken empathy, like soldiers on the battlefield who know what their comrades are thinking just from a glance.

Dogs and men lived a nomadic life, tied to the flock. Though some dogs did choose humans to become their most revered companions, most preferred the smell and company of sheep. But sheepherder and dog came to know each other's hearts and minds in a very special way.

Walk into a dog lover's home today and you will be hard-pressed to find that special kind of relationship in action. Freed from hardship and servitude, our dogs slowly morphed from business partners to beloved companions, with little purpose save amusing us and providing us with affection and loyalty.

Masters of adaptation, they have excelled at this, too. Yet in the heart of every dog remains that running dream, and the elemental drive to perform. It is there for the herders, for the terriers, for the hound—even the tiniest, pampered lapdog with a pink bow tied around its coiffed neck dreams that secret dream.

But when our dogs wake up today, the running dream remains just that, and many of them wonder what haunts them in the night, like some forgotten, scent-filled legend. And what of us? What have we forgotten? The hardships, the simplicities, the frankness, to be sure, among so many other things. But when it comes to our dogs, we have slowly forgotten who they once were, and what they stood for over the ages. We have taken them into our homes and loved them, given them comforts and praise, written books about them, cooked for them, elevated them. Admirable things, all deserved.

We have done something else; we have forgotten their truer natures, and what we once meant to them. We have abandoned an essential empathy that once existed between herder and collie, hunter and spaniel, soldier and mastiff, and replaced it with a new, surrogate construct. Without their permission, we have re-created our dogs in our own image, and they have become to us our own sweet sons and daughters, to be indulged and loved unconditionally, without expectation save companionship. We have made them into proxy humans, and in doing so taken away everything doggish, not only from them, but from ourselves as well. We have turned our backs on a sophisticated, many-centuries-old partnership and replaced it with perpetual parenthood.

Disconnected

The indulgent tendencies of today's typical dog owner have inadver-tently inspired a growing disconnect between people and dogs, and an escalation of unwelcome pet behaviors. I have seen it a thousand times: a passionate person, hard working, too busy for family or friends, falls in love with a puppy and brings it home. A toy breed, perhaps a Shih Tzu or Lhasa Apso. Here is a needy creature, a sociable little love monkey who offers unconditional affection day or night; who could resist returning that love? The dog becomes a surrogate child, and the center of attention; then the mistakes begin.

As the pup grows she becomes the focal point of the owner's affec-tions, demanding attention at will. The dog sleeps in the owner's bed, eats his food, decides when to come or go, initiates all interactions. Little reliable training is given. The pet never earns anything, but instead is given whatever she wants, gratis. Like a dysfunctional trust fund heiress, the dog quickly learns to steer the ship.

When guests come over she barks and jumps up on them repeatedly until they relent and pet her. The owner does nothing because he recognizes no problem; the dog is just an impetuous child happily acting out. The guests smile meekly and secretly wonder if the dry cleaner will be able to get the mud stains out of their gabardine.

Two years later the now-obese dog bites a neighbor's child when the child tries to pick up a dropped cookie on the kitchen floor. The dog gets the cookie and the child gets twelve stitches and a lifelong fear of dogs, while the owner gets the bill and loses a friend.

This person should have a cat, not a dog. Cats are low maintenance, self-sufficient, reclusive, introspective; a step away from the wild, where life is quiet, structured, solitary. A cat can be idolized and pampered without behavioral consequences; they don't need to be walked, or be part of a team.

Cats bear us gracefully, but dogs need mentors, coaches, CEO's. They need us, need to look in our eyes and see strength, security and affirmation. They need to be *understood*. Cats are mysterious, self-reliant works of art, but dogs remain eager members of a larger club, and need more, much more. However, the indulgent dog owner can't tell the difference and, in treating his dog like a cat, he creates a dysfunction he cannot sense.

He is *not* a natural dog owner.

That evening the dog climbs onto his owner's lap as he watches television. They look at each other. "I'm sorry that little girl scared you, Precious," he says, petting the dog's head, thinking he knows his dog.

It's not only naïve owners who rationalize this type of disconnected interaction. Increasingly, in an attempt to appease love-struck owners, a number of trainers and behaviorists have begun to support the humanization of dogs.

A while back I spoke with a self-proclaimed dog trainer based in Los Angeles about the leadership instinct in dogs, and whether or not it was an "old-school" idea in need of rethinking. She insisted that domestic dogs were nothing like their wolf cousins, and were in fact completely adapted to domestic life, with the same motivations as humans regarding needs and desires.

"Dogs choose to sleep in the owner's bed because it's more comfortable than the floor," she said knowingly, her portly, sweater-clad Boston Terrier poured across her lap, growling softly, its eyes ready to burst from its skull. "It has nothing to do with pack status. It's all about logic. Dogs are logical, just like us."

I gracefully extricated myself from the conversation without initiating an unwinnable argument, and without strangling her orc-like Boston. But she and other enablers like her are as we speak spreading this "humanist" style of training to the unsuspecting owners of troubled dogs, and they are eating it up like spilled kibble in a home filled with unneutered Rottweilers. Imagine never having to train a dog to mind, focus, or act civilly. Makes ownership easy, provided you never have guests over.

A trend to treat dogs as if they were human beings is on the rise. This couldn't be more unfair to a dog, who has species-specific characteristics undeniably different from humans—characteristics which need to be *respected*. To pretend a Pekingese is a human child does it a great disservice, and puts a burden on its ability to effectively integrate into our world.

Consider this startling fact: in Seattle, Washington, there are approximately 90,000 children, and over *120,000* dogs. Similar numbers can also be found in San Francisco and other progressive cities. That a city in the United States could have more dogs than children is an astonishing new demographic, one which points to a growing trend of pets replacing kids.

And why not? Pets are more independent and far less of a financial burden. They demand less attention over time, and mature into "adulthood" in just a few years. Even puppies have excellent mobility, and can be taken care of by others, if need be, to facilitate a vacation. They need not be nursed, and can be reliably potty trained within a month or two. Dogs are more interactive, give an immediate emotional return, won't go to college or get addicted to drugs, won't stay out all night with your car—they are simply an easier alternative for young, upwardly mobile persons looking for love but too involved in shaping their own lives to bother with kids.

Empty nesters also make up a large percentage of today's dog owners. Recently abandoned by their grown children, they often fill that emotional void with a dog, and lavish it with the parental love once reserved for their kids, now off to college or on their own. Behavioral problems resulting from this massive onslaught of unconditional love and attention cannot be overstated. Believe me, I know.

Take a look in the yellow pages under *"Dog."* You'll find not only kennels, breeders, veterinarians, pet stores and the like, but also doggy day cares and massage, canine counselors, doggy bakeries and restaurants, pooch parks, custom clothing for dogs, dating and party services, and even dog psychics. Is all of this for them, or for us?

Ineffective owners give pets parity in the home, and often treat them as surrogate children. Rather than help the dog integrate, they simply pretend that they are both kindred human souls cut from the same genetic cloth. In doing so they confound their dogs, and lose hope of ever gaining the intuitive canine sense that effective owners take for granted.

Make no mistake, your dog possesses the same pack instincts as his wolf cousins. Be he a Malamute or Maltese, the desire to belong to a well-led, successful group is as inherent to him as it is to the wolf.

In a perfect world, your dog's social status should be below that of the "two-foots" in his pack. This is not an insult; this is *natural*. Those who think that domestic pack status is passé are applying stilted human logic to the canine equation. It's unfair, and prejudicial. The dog *wants* to look to you for guidance, just as wolves of low rank do with higher-ranked pack animals. When this happens, good behaviors follow naturally. The dog behaves not because it is forced to, but because it *wants* to.

By ignoring the dog's innate desire to be led, owners inadvertently force their dogs to become the leaders of their own "packs," creating all manner of behavioral problems. Without a leader to look up to, your dog takes charge, and can become pushy, controlling, or even aggressive.

This was never an issue for the Basques or their herding dogs. Though mutual respect existed, never was there a question of who was in charge. If there had been any doubt, the dogs would have stopped herding sheep and started killing them instead.

Though old, the herding instinct pales in comparison to the prey instinct. In fact, herding behavior is simply a modification of the instinct to hunt down and kill prey. Instead of killing, Border Collies, Australian Shepherds and Great Pyrenees redirect their desire to kill into a desire to collect, control, protect and covet. Owners of domestic herding dogs see this behavior often, in their dogs' desires to steal and hide pieces of clothing, in their penchant to "herd" children around the yard by nipping at their feet, or in their insatiable desire to chase cars or joggers.

Without the leadership, succor and guidance of their Basque masters, those collies and shepherds would have eventually started killing their charges. They did not, because the Basques had a natural, empathetic understanding of the dog/owner relationship that their dogs instinctively respected. Though more valuable to the Basque than any fifty sheep, a dog that started killing merinos would have lost all usefulness and either been sold or killed outright: very utilitarian, very frank, very doggish. It wasn't fear that kept the dogs in check so much as it was confidence in knowing what their world expected of them.

The Natural Dog Owner

Some dogs are just plain more likable than others; but why?

Apart from heredity, deep-seated psychological scars or breed-specific idiosyncrasies, the causes of unwanted behavior in dogs tends more toward nurture and not nature. And just who are the nurturers? Excluding the first few weeks of a puppy's life, that honor goes to the dog owner. Clearly, just as some parents succeed where others fail, some dog owners are better equipped to raise dogs than others. This begs the question: why *are* some dog owners better at it than others? Are they smarter, bigger, more intimidating? Do they have better facilities? Do their dogs come from superior breeding stock? Is it the food they feed? In a word, no. Owners of well-mannered, thoughtful dogs are not mystical Übermenschen possessing the ability to control animals the way a Tarzan or Dr. Doolittle might. Nor are they necessarily blessed with good fortune, the perfect dog-raising environment, or the best of breeding stock. So just what magical qualities *do* they have that others do not?

The answer is what I call *effective canine empathy*. Like the Basques, successful dog owners adopt a natural, unaffected interpretation of canine behavior, and apply this insight to daily situations. They have the intuitive ability to sense what dogs need or want, why dogs do what they do, and how to get dogs to behave in an agreeable manner, without undue conflict or argument. They understand what dogs are saying with their body language and behavior, and can communicate in a like manner to their dogs. When conflict does occur, they do not fear it; rather, they look upon it as an opportunity to teach and clarify. Successful dog owners simply identify with canines more intimately than do less experienced individuals, who, though ardent in their love for dogs, do not understand issues *in canine terms*.

Effective owners, rather than attempting to turn their dogs into cats or proxy humans, instead *turn themselves into proxy dogs*. This is the key factor in achieving the goal of a well-mannered, confident, thoughtful pet.

Great dog owners also do something else that failed owners do not. They refuse to rhapsodize over their pets, or elevate them to cult status. There is no sugary gush, no acting as if dogs hold a mystical key to their inner wild child. Effective owners know this to be as sophomoric as a middle school romance, and avoid it for the good of the relationship. In its place exists the respectful, calm realization that dogs are not celebrities, carnival rides or furry shamans, but simply marvelous subordinates whose aspirations must take a back seat. It is a composed, mature, ritualistic rapport, and that's the way dogs *want* it. From this emerges a type of elemental love only natural dog owners and their dogs can comprehend.

Are effective dog owners born, not made? Though some certainly are blessed with an intuitive "dog" sense, experience, education and a desire to succeed are all one needs to become a highly effective dog owner.

No dog is perfect, but some come darned close. You know the dogs I'm talking about: they're the ones who smile a lot, who have a sweet, studied calmness about them, who think their way through a situation instead of letting circumstances get the best of them. They are attentive without being pushy, curious without being a bother. They are not afraid of strangers but can tell the good people from the bad. Good dogs have a playful, mischievous side, yet know when it's time to be serious or respectful. And they can always sense when you are upset, happy or sick. Good dogs have a sentient sparkle in their eyes that says: "*Life is good here with you, dog.*" When you meet dogs like these, look to their owners, for they are the ones this book is about. They are the ones to model.

Be the Dog

Just what does "*Be the Dog*" mean? Certainly not getting down on all fours and eating Stroganoff from a bowl beside your poodle. What it does mean is striving to smell, hear, see, taste and touch your world as your dog might, as well as understanding canine body language and being able to second-guess how your dog will react to an impending situation, such as an approaching stranger at a park, a new pair of leather oxfords on the carpet, or a looming thunderstorm. It means understanding how important social interactions are to both dogs and humans. It means establishing yourself as a benevolent manager and taking on the responsibilities of that manager, among them providing food, shelter, safety, purpose, a reliable social structure, intellectual and physical stimuli, and many other components which will be discussed later. It means understanding the canine desires to belong, control, covet. And above all, it means acting in a confident, competent manner, and being as consistently fair as possible in the dog's eyes.

That "trainer" in Los Angeles had few of these qualities, and showed her naïveté by absentmindedly petting her territorial Boston terrier *while the dog was growling.* She showed a stunning lack of canine empathy by not understanding how petting her dog while it performed an antisocial, undesirable behavior was in effect *reinforcing* that behavior. She had trained her dog to be an aggressive little creep, a bitchy little brat in a fur coat.

Her motivation at that moment was a classic blunder: thinking the dog was growling out of concern for its safety, she petted it in an attempt to calm and console. Exactly what you would do with a human child. But that's not the way a dog's mind works; if they are praised for a behavior, they *will repeat that behavior*, plain and simple.

When a dog jumps up on a guest, for instance, the usual reaction of the guest, who doesn't want to be rude, is to meekly pet the dog as it leaps and licks away like some uncontrollable dervish. The perfunctory pet on the head reinforces the jumping behavior, insuring its repetition.

Another example of nonexistent canine empathy occurs when a dog, be it in a home or car, begins barking at strangers walking by. Thinking that the dog is afraid, an owner that pets and comforts the dog in an attempt to alleviate the fear and stop the behavior is, unfortunately, simply reinforcing the undesirable behavior. The solution is a combination of techniques, including long-term socialization (something the owner probably hadn't done), positive reinforcement for *not* barking, and a nonthreatening rebuke as soon as the offending behavior begins. Included, also, should be teaching the dog the "Quiet" command, which could be used to effectively shut down the behavior.

The "Natural"

So, are effective dog owners born, not made? Some are, I think. You know the archetype; a sage old grandpa with a thousand stories who lives on a farm with his wife of fifty years and three easy-going shepherd mixes who all seem to answer to the name "Duke." Big, slow dogs who live easy and take off-leash walks with their owner through the woods on crisp spring mornings. He is attentive to them, but hasn't made the dogs the center of his world. He is more of a big dog brother than a doting day care worker, and the dogs appreciate that. They know he has bigger issues to worry about than their immediate happiness, and that *comforts* them.

Yet with a word or whistle he can get those lumbering dogs running to him from clear across a field. He enjoys the walks as much as the dogs do, not just for the companionship, but for the sights, sounds and scents the dogs share. He enjoys watching them sense what he cannot, and learns about his environment through them. They are *sharing* life.

He knows his dogs' strengths and weaknesses. He makes sure the arthritic eldest of the three doesn't try to follow the youngest up a steep muddy embankment, but doesn't make an issue out of it. He lets them establish their own hierarchy, and steps in only to prevent injury. But that never happens; they are too content to bicker.

Of the generations of dogs he has mentored, none have ever been treated like pampered children, but instead like respected companions. They have had other dogs to interact with, as well as a cadre of adults and children, always around, growing, changing, enriching their lives and teaching them the real meaning of family.

The dogs turn every minute or so to make sure he is still there, and when he finally heads back for the house, they return with him. The very thought of an unmanageable behavior problem among these dogs seems foolish at best.

Education and the drive to empathize are the keys to natural dog ownership. And that is the purpose of this book. In it, I provide you with the seven most important secrets a dog owner can possess and practice, secrets that successful dog owners take for granted. From selection, technique and pack dynamics to owner attitude and purpose, the book will tutor you in every aspect of effective ownership, and explain in clear terms how to connect with your "inner canine." In effect, I will show you how to "*Be the dog.*"

The "Natural" Versus the "Coddler"

On the following page, let's look at an example of effective versus ineffective owner decisionmaking. Here we present two different owners attempting to manage the same situation with their dogs; one chooses the right solution, the other, the wrong one.

SCENARIO #1

Grace walks her Bichon Frise "Gucci" down the same street every morning before going to work. On this morning they turn a corner and are surprised by a group of kids walking to school. Gucci barks at the kids who, undaunted, ask if they can pet her. Shunning the kids, Grace drags Gucci away by the leash, then scoops the dog up into her arms. "It's okay, Gucci," she repeats over and over, backing away and petting the dog's head to comfort her. Amused, the kids walk off.

SCENARIO #2

Pam walks her Bichon Frise "Happy" down the same street each morning before going to work. On this morning they turn a corner and are surprised by a group of kids walking to school. Happy barks at the kids who, undaunted, ask if they can pet her. "Good morning, Tommy," Pam says confidently, recognizing the neighbor's boy, then greeting him with a handshake. "Want to give Happy a cookie?"

"Sure," he says, taking the treat from Pam. Happy has stopped barking and appears attentive and alert.

"Ask him to sit first," she whispers. Tommy asks Happy to sit, and Happy obeys. Tommy then gives Happy the cookie, which he hungrily accepts.

"Go on and pet him when he's done eating, Tommy," Pam says, all tension in the dog's leash relaxed. He does, and soon Happy is luxuriating in a good head rub. Pam gives cookie bits to several of the kids, who each repeat the process. Happy gladly accepts the cookies and the attention. Then the kids continue on their way. Happy wonders if he will see the kids again tomorrow.

Same breed, same situation, totally different outcome. In the first scenario, Grace is as alarmed as Gucci at the sudden appearance of the kids who, though apparently harmless, seem to intimidate both dog *and* owner. Instead of greeting the kids confidently, Grace worriedly drags Gucci away then picks her up and pets her on the head.

Nothing could have been worse. In just those few seconds, Grace succeeded in teaching Gucci:

- **Whenever unexpected events occur, be afraid and run away.**
- **There is no confident "pack leader" in charge.**
- **When you show fear you will be praised with a pat on the head (thereby reinforcing the fearful behavior).**
- **When the leash tightens, something bad is going to happen.**
- **Incessant barking is an acceptable behavior.**
- **Show fear aggression and your problems will go away.**

In the second scenario, Pam shows a better understanding of the situation. Though generally a friendly dog, Happy is a small breed, and can sometimes feel a bit intimidated by crowds of unpredictable children. So when Happy barks, Pam pays little attention, and instead remains calm and interactive. As a confident leader should, she makes first contact, showing Happy that the kids are acceptable and harmless. Happy picks up on this. Pam makes sure to keep a loose leash because she understands how prolonged leash tension can signal a dog that its owner is nervous. Then Pam turns the situation into an educational opportunity by having Tommy reward Happy for sitting, with cookies she was smart enough to keep in her pocket. Once this occurs, the fear potential for the dog is defused, and all is fine. Happy learns that kids can be a source of pleasure, not fear. *Canine* logic at its best. Pam is a natural.

One owner chose well, the other poorly. By understanding the dog's perspective, Pam was able to turn a potentially negative experience into a positive one. Grace, unfortunately, managed only to teach Gucci that kids are to be feared, and that leaders are weak. *Human* logic at its worst. Grace is a coddler.

Dogs Can't Spell Democracy

Recently, great strides have been taken toward making the lives of domestic pets safer and more fulfilling. Animal control officers help dogs and cats whenever they can, enforcing animal cruelty laws enacted to prevent owners from mistreating or ignoring their pets. Veterinary procedures have improved by leaps and bounds, as have preventive vaccination programs. Pet welfare organizations have revolutionized the way we treat dogs, cats and other pets, particularly strays in need of homes. Knowledge of proper pet nutrition has expanded. As mentioned before, we have dog parks dotting the landscape, providing our pooches with controlled spaces in which to run free, and doggy day care facilities, for owners who wish not to leave their pets at home alone all day. Truly, from a dog's perspective, these are the golden days.

We have also begun to apply the idea of basic "civil" rights to animals. Using dogs and cats in medical experimentation has become a hotly contested issue, as has the use of animals in product testing. More humane training and behavior modification methods have been developed and adopted. Even pet health insurance has become popular. All wonderful things, all long overdue.

Some pet advocates have in my opinion begun to push the envelope too far, taking many of the rights we humans enjoy and applying them to dogs and cats, blurring the species-specific differences between us. Many advocates even refuse to recognize the term "owner," instead using the term "guardian." Others claim that dogs have the right not to be trained to perform behaviors they might not otherwise choose to perform naturally.

I'm not in this camp. I'm certainly not yet ready to let my neighbor's spaniel decide who will be the next mayor of my town, and I don't know if I'd be willing to pay pet support to an ex-partner who was lucky (or unlucky) enough to get custody of an old cat or dog.

Seriously, dogs can't spell democracy. It's just not in their vocabulary. If two dogs are in a room and a lamb chop falls on the floor, the stronger, more dominant dog *will* eat it, not share. That's dog life.

Dogs do learn to develop a sense of fairness within their own family group, but they cannot understand abstract terms, and as such don't respond well to rule by committee. Instead, they recognize the leadership hierarchy as the preferable method of governance. And it has worked perfectly well for a million years; as evidence, consider that, next to humans and rodents, canines have spread farther around the planet than any other mammalian species.

When the alpha wolf gets first dibs on a preferred mate, he doesn't run it by a committee first, or share the privilege. He makes the decision and the others live with it, until he's too old to enforce the status quo.

If your dog gets out the door and runs for the street, you *have* to get that dog back into the house before it gets killed. You do not have the option of reasoning or pleading with him; he simply must recognize your authority and obey your command to come back. That's authoritarian, not democratic.

We love our own kids dearly and increasingly let them make choices, to learn how to become independent. But when they are small, it's still our responsibility to make all the important calls. They don't have the ability to choose their own doctor, determine what family rules they will or will not abide by, or decide whether or not to come inside for dinner. As adult dogs have the intellectual capacity of a two-year-old human child, they shouldn't be given those choices either.

What we should give them is a sense of competence, inclusion and purpose, and a feeling that the important things have been taken care of. A dog that has food, shelter, family, guidance and purpose will feel relaxed and happy, as opposed to a dog allowed to do whatever it wants.

Think that LA woman's Boston terrier is happy? Think again; he's miserable. He's always on edge, because, lacking the confidence that emanates from a competent, empathetic owner, he thinks he needs to lead his pack. Though barely twelve inches high, he thinks he must initiate everything. So when a stranger approaches, he growls and gets petted for it. When a child tries to pick up a ball from the floor, he bites. Like a feral child, he's leaderless, and incapable of effective communication. His owner, by appeasing and enabling, has created a creepy, nervous little tyrant. No; dogs don't respond well to democracy, but they do to enlightened leadership, and that's what you should give your dog.

Fitting Old Ways into New Digs

No one wants to rush out into the wilderness with his Chihuahuas and start hunting cougar. That's not what I mean by turning yourself into a proxy dog, or developing effective canine empathy. What owners should strive to do, however, is understand what dogs are really like on the inside, and how their age-old instincts needn't be abandoned or ignored. Truly, the "old" canine ways can be adapted to fit into new digs quite nicely. In doing so, they can actually help to improve the quality of your relationship.

The old bonds we had with dogs back when we depended upon them were more mature and respectful than the ones most owners have today. Then, dogs were functional members of a team and expected to toe the line. Today, though treated with more concern for their general welfare, they are for the most part objects of puerile affection and curiosity, freed of responsibility or expectation. They are like intellectuals suddenly transformed into illiterates. The Basque who watched his dogs effortlessly work a flock of two thousand felt admiration and respect for them; the empty nester who watches his Pekingese piddle on the carpet feels something less grand.

A key characteristic of the natural dog owner is the ability to acknowledge a dog's behavioral heritage, and then find a way to incorporate it into modern life. Simply put, you have to honor the dog's ancient need for purpose by discovering or inventing modern-day substitutes for it.

Let's look at the Border Collie again. Centuries of breeding have produced a fine-tuned herding machine, an obsessive/compulsive fanatic capable of controlling hundreds of animals, each five times its size, as if they were guided by the sheer power of the dog's thought waves.

If you haven't watched a Border Collie work, you haven't experienced the essence of purity of form and function. Untiring perfectionists, their hypnotic stare, or "eye," delivered from a distinctive crouching posture, mesmerizes sheep or cattle into submission. Even eight-week-old Border Collie pups with no herding experience at all will assume this position and attempt to herd blowing leaves, ducklings—even flashlight beams.

A working Border Collie runs fifty to a hundred miles every day and solves a myriad of problems along the way, using its intellect and independent nature to succeed. Many studies have shown the Border Collie to be the most intelligent of breeds, with the Poodle and German Shepherd second and third, respectively.

It took over a hundred years of selective breeding to create this work of art. But take this highly-tuned Formula One racer and place it in a placid, "happening-less" home environment, and watch the trouble brew. Boredom and inactivity are anathema to a Border Collie, and can quite literally drive them insane. Biting, antisocial behavior, escaping, destructive behavior, and even euthanasia can result, all because a well-meaning fan did not respect centuries of breeding, and instead tried to turn a Ferrari into a houseplant. This is not *natural*.

The Border Collie is a high maintenance pet that isn't for every dog lover. Those who want to successfully own one must give the dog an outlet for its breeding, and must recognize and respect its uniqueness. Exercise, agility classes, basic and advanced obedience work, early socialization, trick training, herding classes—as much stimulation as possible is needed to occupy this dog's mind, heart and soul. The obsessive herding desire must be replaced with something just as stimulating and purpose-driven. Nipping kids on the ankles or chasing joggers won't do, but regularly retrieving a flying disk or playing flyball just might. Choose to treat this breed like a placid Maltese and you'll be in for a sour surprise.

Few owners understand this. Instead, they apply freethinking human psychology to their dogs and expect them to respond favorably. The Norwich Terrier that has dug a thousand holes in his owner's yard in search of that pesky mole gets at best a perfunctory verbal scolding, despite the fact that, as have terriers for centuries, he is simply doing what his DNA tells him to do. Scolding or whining does nothing; redirecting the behavior by giving the dog a specific spot in which digging is allowed (such as a small sandbox with treats and toys buried in the sand) will work, as will not banishing the dog to the yard all day alone.

Unlike herding breeds, scenthounds obey a different muse. A Beagle for example will follow a scent trail wherever it leads, even out onto a freeway. Better to take her to a dog-friendly park on a long lead and let her track squirrels for an hour, or find cookies hidden around the yard.

So, a key factor in becoming a natural dog owner is the ability to find acceptable, modern alternatives for your dog to express its breed heritage on a regular basis, even if you live in the city. I'll cover this in detail later in the book. For now, know that acknowledging your dog's instincts and finding acceptable avenues for them in everyday life is not only necessary, but immensely fun.

Embracing the Seven Secrets of the Natural Dog Owner

The very fact that you are reading this means you sense some problem in the relationship with your dog. That's good; it means you are done rationalizing, coddling, excusing, condoning, ignoring, apologizing, humanizing and enabling. You think you may have inadvertently turned your dog into an impertinent pre-schooler, and you want out. Excellent. I forgive you. Now let's fix things.

The first step toward becoming a natural dog owner is to recognize your own owner/dog disconnect. The second is to take comfort in knowing that you are not alone. It would not be an exaggeration to say that the majority of dog owners today are just like you, and that the natural dog owner is slowly becoming something of a pariah. Doubt that? Consider the following:

- **Nearly 4.7 million dog bites per year on average are reported in the United States (5 million in 2004, with close to eight hundred thousand of them requiring medical attention).**

- **Each year about twenty persons (mostly children) are killed in dog attacks in the United States alone.**

- **Over one-third of all personal liability claims on home-owner's insurance policies are directly caused by dog attacks or dog destruction.**

These figures point to one unavoidable conclusion: something's amiss in "dogdom." For some reason, a good percentage of dogs are either simply misbehaving, or are so poorly adjusted to their adopted environments that they find it necessary to misbehave. The dog/owner relationship is, in many instances, breaking down.

Experienced trainers and behaviorists agree that aggression or mis-behavior problems in dogs are nearly always caused by owners who either abuse or spoil their dogs. Oddly, these divergent methodologies often produce the same results: an antisocial, aggressive or pushy dog that, due either to misperceptions of fear or dominance, decides to behave badly.

Natural dog owners rarely experience profound behavioral problems with their dogs. Like that kindly grandpa, they take a "dog's-eye view" of things, and as such create an atmosphere of trust and self-assurance in their pets, resulting in few behavioral setbacks. When a dog has a "natural" owner, he obeys *naturally*.

Natural owners do not expect a dog to exhibit human behaviors, but instead want the dog be a dog. That's a huge relief to the pet, who has no idea what being human really means.

Certain owner habits and actions expose the coddler; you need to know if you are one. Where are you on the road between the coddler and the natural? Ask yourself these questions:

Do you plead with your dog, and endlessly repeat commands only to be ignored?

Does your dog sleep in bed with you?

Does your dog growl at you or other friendly humans, for any reason?

Do you have trouble getting your dog to come to you?

Does your dog steal your belongings and fight to keep them?

Do you rationalize your dog's misbehaviors?

When your dog shoves his head into your lap, do you automatically pet him?

Is your dog obese or food-aggressive?

Do you talk baby talk to your dog?

Does your dog use its body to manipulate you and other people?

Are you unable to groom your dog without her growling or biting?

Does your dog bark or whine incessantly?

Is your dog destructive in the home?

Does your adult dog have regular housetraining accidents?

Does your dog suffer from undue separation anxiety?

When you open the front door, does your dog push by you and rush out?

When guests come over, does your dog growl at them, jump on them, huddle close to you or hide?

Do you walk your dog, or does he walk you?

If you answered yes to more than a few of these, odds are you are a coddler, and are trying to turn your dog into a proxy human. Truth is, you've got a furry pre-schooler with big teeth and an attitude running your life, and some strange part of you *likes it*. That is the self-interested needy part, the part that isn't truly concerned with the dog's well being. A natural dog owner wouldn't do that. *A natural dog owner never puts his or her thirst for companionship and recognition above the basic needs of the dog.*

Go back and reread the questions above. Now ask yourself; could a dog like that really be *happy*? I think you know the answer.

The Magnificent Seven

Part Two of the book is coming up. It is dedicated to detailing each of the Seven Secrets of the Natural Dog Owner, and to showing you how to integrate them into life with your dog. By doing so, you will gradually develop your own sense of canine empathy, allowing you to see things from the dog's-eye view.

Things will slowly change; you will see why your dog acts the way he does, be able to predict his actions in advance and, if unwanted, head them off at the pass. You will develop an ability to sense your dog's needs and provide them to him *without* coddling. You will not be afraid to confront your dog in responsible, doggish fashion. You will start to feel more like a mentor and less like a butler.

At first your dog will wonder what the heck is going on. He may miss all the gratis attention, the artificial status, the goose-down comforter, the pandering, the enabling. But then, slowly, he will start to develop something unique, something he vaguely remembers having when he first showed up. He will begin to *respect and admire* you. He'll begin to like you again in ways you haven't experienced before. He will see a kindred soul, a doggish two-foot, a natural.

The following is a list of the Seven Secrets. Take a look, then move on to Part Two. But first, go have a quick talk with your dog. Tell him to get ready, because he ain't in Kansas anymore.

The Seven Secrets of the Natural Dog Owner

1. Choose Your Friends Wisely

2. Understand and Apply Leadership,
   the Sacred Canine Code

3. Embrace a Canine Attitude and Awareness

4. Turbocharge Your Dog's IQ

5. Enrich Your Dog's Environment

6. Keep Your Dog Healthy and Safe

7. Endow Your Dog with Purpose

The Seven Secrets of the Natural Dog Owner

Truth be told, the Seven Secrets aren't secretive at all, at least not to natural dog owners, who don't sit home jealously guarding the "sacred dog scrolls." Rather, they simply relate to dogs in a natural, casual, empathetic way, and understand instinctively what to do, how to train, what boundaries to set. No one is keeping secrets; rather, the knowledge has been ignored or abandoned over the years by owners more interested in their dogs' hairstyles than in their behavioral profiles.

The information in Part Two rectifies that. In it I restore forgotten proficiencies, reintroduce dignity to the partnership, and give you a chance to feel, perhaps for the first time, what it is truly like to be an effective member of history's most famous partnership.

Don't think this is simply a retrospective tribute. I don't intend to fully sanctify the past while wholly condemning the present. Far from it; the past contained callous, often brutal treatment of dogs, and conditions that shortened and trivialized dogs' lives. The Seven Secrets combine yesterday's empathies with today's sympathies, creating a fusion of philosophies that teaches, protects, and normalizes.

Before you begin, take your dog for a night walk. Watch her interact with the environment; notice how she relates to you. Moreover, try to perceive things yourself; sniff the air, look at the trees, feel the wind. Guess at what she is thinking. Begin to become aware.

Choose Your Friends Wisely

Not all dogs are created equal.

There, I said it. Does this mean that some dogs are intrinsically better than others? That's a subjective decision left up to you. But for me, some dogs have the magic, and some don't. Just realize that you have the right to decide for yourself whether or not you "like" a dog's personality, physical characteristics, and behavioral profile. Trust me; when you meet the right one, you'll know.

Breeds

One hundred and fifty distinct breeds are currently recognized by the American Kennel Club (AKC), with hundreds more established and registered throughout the world. In no other species can such a level of physical and behavioral diversity be found. Remarkable, if you consider that the smallest dog (perhaps a teacup Chihuahua, weighing in at about two to four pounds) and the largest (the Mastiff, at well over two hundred) have the same basic DNA. It would be comparable to one adult human weighing one hundred times as much as another!

Besides profound differences in size and weight, dog breeds display distinctive behaviors and tendencies. Some, like the Border Collie, we have already discussed; others are just as unique. Here's a sample list of a few popular dog breeds, and an abbreviated behavioral profile of each:

Labrador Retriever
Gregarious and willing to work, the Labrador retriever is great with kids. Traditionally used by hunters as a land and water retriever, the "Lab" also has a great nose. Its gentle disposition, love of water and "soft" mouth, all vital to its utility, make for a great family pet for those willing to exercise it regularly.

German Shepherd Dog
Loyal, intelligent, protective, driven and courageous, the German Shepherd Dog (or GSD) is initially reserved with strangers. Developed in late nineteenth-century Germany, the versatile GSD was bred to be a "super dog," capable of doing just about anything. Police and military units often use GSDs for bomb detection and rescue work, and for help in capturing criminals or enemy combatants.

Poodle
Clever, happy, alert and friendly, the poodle is a great family dog with bouncing enthusiasm. Originally bred in Germany to flush and retrieve waterfowl, they have great noses and love the water.

Rottweiler
Powerful, protective, territorial and suspicious of strangers, today's Rottweiler is the direct descendent of mastiff-like, Roman herd-guarding dogs. They are loyal, territorial, stubborn, and inherently dominant.

American Staffordshire Terrier (or Pit Bull Terrier)
Though in essence the same breed, some claim the American Staffordshire, or "Amstaff," to be unique, and less aggressive than its infamous pit bull cousin. Powerful and tenacious, the Amstaff possesses a high prey drive, and is loyal to its family. Originally bred in England as the perfect fighting machine, the Amstaff (and most pit bull variances) are the result of crossing nineteenth century bulldog blood with various ter-

rier stock. This energetic, tenacious breed retains many of its pugilistic instincts, and must have its strong prey drive kept in check.

Shih Tzu

Though small, this cheerful breed is sturdier than many other toys. The Shih Tzu is playful, active, and usually welcoming to strangers. Originally bred in China, the Shih Tzu's job was to bark when strangers approached. Though it has become a classic companion/lap dog, it retains some of its ancient feisty nature, but can be sensitive to heavy-handed training.

Beagle

Athletic and scent-driven, the beagle is robust, friendly and vocal. This medium-sized hound was originally bred to track rabbit and other small game. Stubborn and easily distracted by scent, the beagle has a sweet disposition, and needs early training and lots of exercise. And they bark!

All popular, and all very distinct. The Shih Tzu for instance could not be more different than the GSD in both size and behavior. The Shih Tzu, bred to be a companion dog, is nowhere near as athletic or protective as the GSD. The GSD has a fantastic sense of smell, while the Shih Tzu, with its short nasal cavities, rates low on the "sniffer" scale. The GSD, because of its power, courage and high prey drive, has been used for decades as a police and military dog; the Shih Tzu wouldn't know what to do with a bad guy.

Do these two dogs differ in terms of ownership? Heck yes! The Shih Tzu owner can live a relatively sedate life with a Shih Tzu; some basic training, a walk or two, a quick romp in the yard and a daily brushing are all it needs. It can be taken with ease on trips, and fits into even the smallest of homes or apartments. The GSD? Better have your running shoes and a dominant disposition handy. The GSD needs a physically competent and consistent leader, early and continued training, and an outlet for its intelligence and athleticism. And GSDs need constant socialization to prevent territorial aggression later in life. Definitely *not* the breed for a laid-back, homebound owner, or someone intending to spoil their dog. The Shih Tzu is a low-maintenance compact car, the GSD, a high-maintenance racer.

Those in the market for a new dog need to see the selection process as more than just an esthetic, "point-and-click" experience, or an impulsive, guilt-ridden rescue mission. A dog after all is not a hamster, which lives for two or three years, can't fetch slippers, smile, or shake your hand. Dogs are dynamic, social creatures, and the one you choose will be with you for a good long while. Why not shoot for the best marriage possible?

The natural owner chooses a dog carefully, without esthetic prejudice or emotion. Secret One explains how proper selection can set the tone for the relationship, and then teaches readers how to properly select a pet. For those who already own a dog, the importance of learning as much as possible about its background is discussed, as are environmental and attitudinal adjustments needed to best fit the dog.

Why Selection Matters

Why do so many dog breeds exist? After all, the number of recognized cat breeds hovers around forty, many fewer than the hundreds of dog breeds found throughout the world. Why? Because cats, though certainly beautiful and fun, have traditionally served but one utilitarian purpose: ratting. That's it. No tracking, retrieving or herding (the mind boggles); just keeping the rat population out of grain supplies and shipboard provisions.

You don't need forty different cat breeds to kill rats. Rather, the variance in cat breeds arose not out of utility, but solely out of the esthetic aspirations of breeders, who might wish to produce a lithe cat with a short brown coat, or a sturdy cat with a long black coat. Though temperament and size vary somewhat from breed to breed, domestic cats' physical and behavioral profiles vary little in comparison to those of dogs.

Another factor in the discrepancy between cat and dog breeds is the length of time each species has been domesticated. Developed primarily from small African and European wildcats, the domestic cat has been selectively bred by humans for perhaps five thousand years. The domestic dog, with roots in the wolf, has been genetically manipulated by us for twenty times that.

Because of their intelligence, pack structure and adaptability, dogs became useful servants to us perhaps as long as one hundred thousand years ago. The gradual diversification of breeds occurred because of our differing needs; protection, watchdog, herding, hunting, ratting, tracking—selective breeding over the centuries morphed canines into whatever we needed them to be. Their utility was the magic wand that made the beagle so different from the Irish wolfhound, the Corgi so unlike the Siberian Husky. Over the millenia, a plethora of breeds appeared, each custom-made for a specific job. Only in the last two hundred years has esthetics become a major factor in the selective breeding of dogs.

Because of this focused specialization, some breeds have developed a somewhat narrow "utility;" they became so proficient at one thing that they lost uncle wolf's penchant for overall adaptability. The pit bull, for instance, became such a good dog fighter that it lost much of its natural aptitude to socialize with other dogs. The Border Collie developed such an obsession for herding that it lost the capacity to simply relax and leave "management and inventory control" to humans.

This narrowing of utility makes some dog breeds incompatible with certain lifestyles, and with certain owners. For instance, an eighty-year-old arthritic retiree might not want to try keeping a high-strung hunting breed such as a Visla or Weimaraner in her studio apartment in Brooklyn. The reason is twofold: First, the dog would lose its mind for lack of exercise and purpose. Second, the frail owner would lose control of such active, domineering breeds, and would eventually find herself at the bottom of the "pack," resulting in all manner of misbehavior.

Years ago I received a call from a slight elderly woman who, upon the death of her husband, was given a male Rottweiler puppy by her son-in-law, who felt she needed companionship and protection. What a gaffe! Rottweilers are powerful, dominant animals in need of not only exercise but early training, and a no-nonsense owner unafraid of establishing his or her dominance.

By the time the dog was six months old, it was bigger than the befuddled woman and five times as strong. She simply could not train it or even walk it. To make matters worse, the dog had been purchased from a "backyard breeder," who sold puppies for profit in the classifieds. Notorious for being over-bred because of popularity, "backyard" Rotts often display profound physical and behavioral problems, especially when bred by irresponsible profiteers.

This Rott was a behavioral and physiological train wreck—bad hips, poor overall conformation, and a profoundly fearful disposition toward strangers and other dogs. Just imagine this poor, terrified senior being dragged by him down a busy street! He'd already bitten two people and was beginning to growl and nip at her; something had to be done to prevent her from getting sued, or worse.

I didn't waste my time trying to educate her or train the dog. She simply did not have the mettle to handle him. Luckily, I was able to find a Rottweiler rescue organization willing to take him in. I did not return him to the breeder, who bred Rott puppies like gerbils, selling them in the paper for one-fifth the price of a well-bred Rott. After threatening to report him to animal control, he did agree to refund a portion the money. If returned to him, the poor flawed animal would have gone on to sire litters of psychotic, fear-biting, untrainable puppies.

After discussing the situation with the flustered, guilt-ridden woman, she agreed to adopt an easy-going adult Maltese from a rescue club. No fear-biting, no dragging her down the street, no intimidation. She simply had no business owning a behaviorally challenged Rottweiler, and was better off with a placid, low-energy dog.

This principle applies to all of us; we too can obtain the wrong dog and then spend years fighting breed-specific or personality issues. For instance, a physically-imposing owner with a deep voice and a commanding presence might do better than to choose a small, shy, submissive dog, who would in all likelihood be intimidated by the owner's daunting presence. Or, a family with children might have trouble if they chose a Chow Chow, a breed with a history of intolerance toward children.

How the Home Environment Helps Determine Selection

When I speak of the "home environment," I'm not just referring to the physical parameters of the home. True, the availability of a fenced yard and the square footage of the home can both play a significant role in the selection process. But the environment consists of more than just physical space. It includes other "pack" members and their personalities, the overall energy level of the household, neighborhood characteristics, and the dog's access to stimulating activities.

How big a home is has less of an effect upon a dog's happiness than one might think. I've seen Great Danes, Greyhounds, Bullmastiffs and other big breeds get along just fine in apartments, and Jack Russell Terriers, Australian Shepherds and Pointers go nuts in three-bedroom homes.

Size alone does not determine space requirements. Rather, breed-specific personality traits are often the deciding factor. The Great Dane, for instance, though huge, tends to be laid back and lazy while in the home, making it a decent choice for those with limited space. Bred as a guard dog, it does not need a large area to feel useful. The Weimaraner, however, bred to hunt, needs more space to feel at ease.

In general, dogs bred to hunt, retrieve, herd or track need a decent-sized home environment. Toy and companion breeds, sighthounds, mastiff-type breeds and most terriers can do well in smaller homes.

Exceptions abound, however. Though a guarding breed, Rottweilers need space, due in part to their heritage as a herd-guarder. Boxers, Siberian Huskies and Doberman Pinschers also need plenty of space. Though in the sporting group, spaniels and retrievers can get by in smaller environs provided they receive daily exercise. Though scent-hounds, the Dachshund, Beagle, Bassett Hound, and Petit Basset Griffon Vendeen are also easily kept in apartments.

Sighthounds are an odd bunch. Bred to run fast to catch hare, small gazelle and other game, they tend toward the large side. Given their speed potential, one would think they'd need a football field-sized back-yard and a palatial home. Not so; provided they are taken for regular romps, sighthounds love to laze around the home, rarely getting overly frisky or rambunctious. It's why rescue Greyhounds make such good apartment dogs.

Big lumbering Mastiff-type breeds such as the Bullmastiff, Great Dane and Saint Bernard can do well in smaller homes provided they receive daily exercise. Bred to be somewhat sedentary, they lazily guard an owner's property and immobilize an intruder until the owner arrives. This makes them adaptable to smaller confines.

As toys were designed to be companion dogs, they require less space than other breeds, and thrive in apartments or small homes. A yard for these dogs is a luxury, not a necessity. Owners of Miniature Pinschers, Affenpinschers and Toy Manchester Terriers, though, will need to provide their frisky pets with a higher level of activity to soothe their livelier natures.

Small to medium-sized terriers do well in small homes provided they receive ample exercise each day. Larger terriers, though, won't fare as well. American Staffordshire Terriers (or pit bulls), Staffordshire Bull Terriers (essentially miniature AmStaffs), Airedales, and Kerry Blue Terriers will all fare better in larger homes with fenced yards. All terriers, though, require more exercise than size would indicate.

Who's at Home?

The natural dog owner chooses a dog that will best get along with whoever lives in or frequents the home. If you have young children, for instance, it wouldn't be a great idea to choose a Chinese Shar-pei, Chow Chow, Akita, Great Pyrenees, Kuvasz or Komondor, as these breeds tend to prefer more controlled, predictable home environments. They can be intolerant of a little person's spontaneity and penchant for pulling on ears and tails. Though these breeds can certainly become accustomed to your own children, the problem lies with their inability to accept and tolerate your children's friends, who will certainly visit regularly. Dog breeds that tend toward the more serious side do better in homes without kids, and with owners who early on establish themselves as capable leaders.

Herding dogs such as the Border Collie often have problems with small children in the home. They can take issue with the uncontrolled actions of kids, and end up attempting to herd them, often nipping in the process. They will also chase children who run by, or who ride bicycles. It's not true aggression, but just an expression of their need to organize and control.

Though toy breeds can be great with kids, they are inherently careful about getting hurt. A Chihuahua, for example, can be seriously injured by a troop of kids who run into a room and accidentally fall onto the poor dog. For this reason, toys can sometimes bite children in an attempt to protect themselves. Natural dog owners always teach their children never to roughhouse, especially with a toy breed.

A list of the AKC dog breeds that fare best in adult homes, sans small children, follows. For those of you who have these breeds, I must reiterate; all of these dogs can get along *perfectly well* with family children if the dogs are properly trained and socialized; it is usually the visiting children who might be at risk.

Afghan Hound

Akita

American Staffordshire Terrier (or pit bull)

Bedlington Terrier

Border Collie

Borzoi

Bouvier des Flandres

Cocker Spaniel

Dalmatian

Giant Schnauzer

Great Pyrenees

Greyhound

Komondor

Kuvasz

Lhasa Apso

Pekingese

Puli

Saluki

Shiba Inu

Staffordshire Bull Terrier

The natural dog owner with children chooses a happy, gregarious breed that not only tolerates children, but welcomes their zany unpredictability. Generally, spaniels (excluding today's Cocker) and retrievers make excellent additions to a home with children, as do many terriers, some dogs from the working group, as well as some toy breeds.

Here is a list of some ideal dog breeds for homes with young children. Again, realize that many breeds not listed can work out fine provided the natural dog owner establishes leadership and socializes the dog well:

All pointer and setter breeds

All retrievers, especially the Golden and Labrador

All spaniels (excluding the Cocker)

Bearded Collie

Bichon Frise

Boston Terrier

Boxer

Bulldog

Corgi (both Cardigan and Pembroke)

French Bulldog

Most hounds, excluding the sighthounds

Most terriers, excluding the pit-bull types, and the Bedlington and Scottish terriers

Most toys (excluding the Chihuahua, Italian Greyhound, Miniature Pinscher, Papillon and Pekingese)

Newfoundland

Poodle

Saint Bernard

An additional word on pit-type breeds; they tend to be simply fantastic with the children in the family. It's visiting kids that can become a serious issue, as well as *any* other neighborhood pets that might happen by unannounced. For these reasons, I tend to advise against them for families with kids, or neighbors with dogs or cats.

What about the German Shepherd Dog, as well as similar breeds like the Belgian Sheepdog, the Belgian Malinois, and the Tervuren? Though all great dogs with unparalleled loyalty to family, their highly protective natures can often make guests feel initially unwelcome. But you will be hard-pressed to find a more loyal, intelligent, protective companion than these.

The same holds true with Rottweilers, who do quite well with family children but can be wary of guests. The Rough Collie, Australian Shepherd and Australian Cattle Dog, while they can be great with kids, also have the herding/nipping issue to contend with.

The bottom line: if you have children, choose a breed or breed-type that has a history of tolerating as much roughhousing, handling and spontaneity as possible, not only from the family brood, but from anyone who happens to visit. Remember: the natural owner, *not the dog*, is in charge of protecting the home. Choose a dog that shows staid suspicion toward strangers and you'll be at risk of a biting incident somewhere down the road.

Yard or Not?

Having a well-fenced yard or dog pen can be a great boon to a natural dog owner. It allows you to let the dog out to relieve himself, or to run around without the need for you to actually don coat and shoes and go out there yourself. This can be a godsend during inclement weather, or when you simply do not have the time to walk your dog. A yard or pen will also allow you to leave your home for periods longer than a dog's housetraining can safely allow it to stay inside.

But a yard or pen is not the panacea most dog owners think. In fact, it can sometimes work against you. Those who get into the habit of putting their dogs out in a yard or pen often become negligent about taking their pets out into the real world, where they can get needed exercise *and* socialization, two vital duties of the natural dog owner. Relying on a yard or pen can also create dubious housetraining habits for dogs that stay out there much of the day. When outside, dogs relieve themselves whenever they choose, and consequently may not develop an "inside versus outside" mentality. The natural dog owner teaches this difference to his or her dog as early on as possible, and maintains it throughout the dog's life; the owner who relegates his or her dog to the yard or pen for most of the day runs the risk of indoor accidents.

The yard or pen also creates an "out of sight, out of mind" mentality. When left to its own devices out there, a dog will often not receive the basic training it needs to be a well-mannered member of the family. Yarded dogs often show their lack of couth by jumping up, digging, barking incessantly, or behaving in a generally antisocial manner. This occurs because of boredom, isolation, and because owners are not present to modify undesirable behaviors when they occur.

Though a yard or pen is handy to have, it should never become a substitute for proper training, socialization, and leadership. Use it; don't abuse it.

Choose a Dog that Emulates Your Persona

I'm often amazed at how similar owners and their dogs appear. A Churchill-like curmudgeon chooses a Bulldog, a Garbo look-alike owns an Afghan hound, a prize-fighter has a Boxer—it really does happen. But, just as often, I run into someone with a distinct personality who has chosen a dog with the exact *opposite* character traits.

There was the slow, steady retiree who bought a high-energy, field-bred Visla; the active young woman who adopted a geriatric Clumber Spaniel; the gregarious single mother of four who fell for a shy, reserved Saluki. When matches like these occur, trouble often follows.

Often the looks of a dog appeal to a person with little knowledge of the dog's actual temperament, or the gravity of the dog's situation might coerce the person into rescuing the animal. Impulse buys, especially when children are present, are another big motivator. For whatever reasons, many owners end up with the wrong dog.

Let's look at that retiree's situation. He'd acquired a rambunctious Visla from a breeder who normally sold puppies to bird hunters. These dogs have limitless energy and a high drive to work; problem is, he lived in a two-bedroom townhouse with his wife, and had an arthritic hip. A laid-back fellow, he simply couldn't keep up with the needs of such a spirited pet. The dog didn't get exercised, and began to act out his frustrations by destroying furniture, peeing on carpets and eating shoes.

This man should have traded dogs with that active young person. He'd have gotten the lethargic Clumber Spaniel, happy with a slow two-block stroll once a day, while the excitable young person would have gotten the Visla, willing to run three miles a day after playing catch for an hour.

And the mom? In such a child-centric home she would have been better off with a child-loving dog, eager to have youngsters hanging from its ears and tail like Christmas tree ornaments. The reserved Saluki was apt to hide under the bed or nip at the annoying kids; better to have had a Labrador or Golden Retriever, Newfoundland or Standard Poodle, all kid-crazy and able to thrive around high levels of unpredictable activity. The Saluki is a better choice for the reserved professional in a quiet, predictable environment, perhaps someone able to jog a few miles per day with the lithe, discerning dog.

The natural dog owner honestly appraises his or her own personality, then selects a dog to best fit that profile. If other persons live in the home, they too must be factored into the selection.

Kids? Get a dog that not only can put up with pandemonium, but flourish in it. Low-energy people in charge? Choose a dog that mirrors that level of activity. Can't keep your running shoes off? Get a dog that can keep pace. Petite, elderly, or physically challenged? Avoid powerful dominant types in favor of a smaller, more docile dog. Pass on the

Rottweiler, Akita or German Shepherd Dog, and consider a Maltese, Soft-coated Wheaten Terrier, Border Terrier, or Bichon Frise, all less dominant breeds easily controlled by owners who'd rather not have to vie for control of the home.

The bottom line: if you are in the market for a dog, be a natural and do your homework. Size up your own persona and that of your family. What are you willing to put up with, and what are you averse to? If you have kids, opt for a happy, sociable breed. Have another dog or a cat? Avoid breed-types known to have high prey drives, and choose a dog that's more apt to accept other animals. Need a dog to accompany you on daily jogs? Avoid short-legged or heavy dogs in favor of natural runners like a Border Collie, Whippet, or Pointer.

Study the breeds and yourself, then make your selection based not on emotion or aesthetics, but on honest common sense.

Choose a Genetically Sound Dog

Though innate behavior is the prime consideration when choosing a dog, a few other more practical issues do merit discussion. Health issues unique to certain breeds should be included in the decision-making process. For instance, here are a few:

- Great Danes and Newfoundlands have a higher incidence of heart disease than other breeds.

- Hip dysplasia, a hereditary condition affecting structure of the hips, occurs with more frequency in German Shepherd Dogs and other large breeds than in smaller dogs.

- Deafness, skin problems and allergies are more common among Dalmatians than other breeds.

- Spaniels and Australian Shepherds show a higher incidence of epilepsy than other breeds.

Breed-specific diseases occur in part because of inbreeding (mating closely related dogs) and line breeding (mating dogs within the same family line, excluding siblings, parents and grandparents), practices used to preserve the most desirable physical and behavioral characteristics of each breed. When two dogs from the same line are bred together, the chances of undesirable recessive genes pairing up in the offspring increases dramatically, leading to the expression of potentially serious medical conditions. It's why caring, conscientious breeders often mate their dogs to champion breed lines far removed from their own. Called crossbreeding, it helps minimize disease and promote breed vigor.

To minimize the chance of your dog having some serious health issues:

- **Research the breeds you like online, specifically breed-specific inherited disorders.**

- **Avoid breeds with significant medical problems, if possible.**

- **Purchase books on breed-specific behavior, but avoid partisan breed books, as they tend to show favoritism toward their own breeds.**

- **Choose a breeder with a sterling reputation, preferably one you have received a favorable reference for. Don't be shy; ask about their breeding practices, and avoid those who mate siblings to siblings, or offspring to their parents or grandparents. Favor those who practice crossbreeding with breeders in other geographic areas.**

- **Avoid rare breeds, as they often have a small gene pool, increasing the odds of inherited disease.**

Longevity

In general, the larger the breed, the shorter its lifespan. Danes, Mastiffs and other giant breeds tend to live a maximum of ten to twelve years, while toy breeds such as the Chihuahua and Yorkshire Terrier can get close to eighteen. In general:

- Dogs over eighty pounds can live between ten and twelve years.
- Dogs between fifty and eighty pounds can live between twelve and fourteen years.
- Dogs between twenty and fifty pounds can live between twelve and sixteen years.
- Dogs under twenty pounds can live between fifteen and eighteen years.

These are broad estimations based upon optimal health, diet and exercise; lifespan will be affected dramatically by diseases such as cancer, arthritis, hip dysplasia and heart disease.

Grooming Issues

One early summer a client of mine adopted a wonderful adult Siberian Husky. After just a few training sessions, dog and owner were getting along perfectly. But the owner was not prepared for the volume of shed hair coming off the dog. Anyone who has owned an arctic breed like the Husky knows how quickly vacuum bags can fill up; the thick double coat literally flies off, especially when temperatures rise. It sounds trivial, but for those who value a clean home, it can become a major issue.

It did for my client; regrettably she decided to give the dog back to the rescue club, and opted for a female boxer with a short, manageable coat. The Husky found a new owner within a week, so everyone was happy.

The lesson is simple: behavior isn't everything. Whatever dog you end up with, be sure you are up to its grooming needs, especially coat maintenance. Breeds with long coats and dense undercoats need daily brushing, and will require you to vacuum the home every day. Long coats mat and tangle easily and wick up disagreeable smells; dogs kept outside for long periods of time will need frequent bathing. Breeds like the Chow Chow, German Shepherd Dog, Siberian Husky, Malamute, Samoyed, Puli, Old English Sheepdog and others fit into this camp.

If you're after low-maintenance grooming, opt for a dog with a short coat, or one that is non-shedding. Boxers, Pugs, Greyhounds, Whippets, Pointers, Beagles, Mastiffs and Bullmastiffs all fit into the shorthaired category; most terriers and Poodles don't shed, but do need regular haircuts. Consider all other selection criteria first however; it makes no sense to have a low-maintenance coat on a high-maintenance dog.

Choosing a Mixed Breed

I love mutts. When I see one walking down the street, I guess at its breed lineage, then ask the owner to see how close I've come. Though I usually come close, occasionally I get a nice surprise, which keeps me guessing. The weird ones, like a Bearded Collie/Whippet mix, or a Mastiff/Brussels Griffon mix—they crack me up.

Breeders are probably rolling their eyes reading this. But the truth is, mixed breeds are charming, smart, affordable and abundant. Most of us, in fact, have owned more mutts than purebreds, if only for the fact that shelters are filled with them, and apart from a neutering/vaccination fee, are free for the taking. Purebreds often cost thousands, making them out of reach for many.

Most natural dog owners know the breeds well enough to identify which have gone into the making of a mutt. It's often a combination of two popular breeds: Labrador or Golden Retrievers, Shepherds, Pit Bulls, Border Collies, Rottweilers, Boxers, Beagles—whichever happen to be the most sought-after breeds of the time and place.

How do these mixes come to pass? Largely through the irresponsibility of owners, unfortunately, who, because they entertain thoughts of one day breeding their dogs, refuse to neuter, then allow their pets to roam and mate with other roamers. The unwanted puppies usually end up in a shelter, hoping for adoption.

There is also the purposeful interbreeding of purebreds by those wishing to create a hybrid pet. Now a popular trend, "designer" dogs such as Labradoodles (Lab/Poodle) and Puggles (Pug/Beagle) sell well primarily because of their unique appearances, and because of effective publicity campaigns. Their breeders, who claim to have higher motivations than simple profit, claim (and rightly so, I think) that some purebred dogs have become genetically inferior due to rampant inbreeding and minuscule gene pools, and that their hybridized pets (read mutts) counter that by creating "hybrid vigor," a broadening of the gene pool which returns a healthy genetic diversity to the mix.

In truth, most mixed-breeds have two purebred parents, and as such aren't all that removed from their genetic history. Nevertheless, I do believe that, on average, mutts are healthier and express fewer hereditary diseases than do purebreds. The oldest dogs I see are invariably mixed-breeds. Conversely, the dogs with the highest incidence of cancers, hip dysplasia and other serious health issues are often rare purebreds.

A mixed-breed dog will readily show physical and behavioral traits common to its parent breeds. A Rottweiler/Lab mix, for instance, will often have the heavy-boned frame of the Rottweiler, while sporting a somewhat smaller head and body. It will sometimes be less territorial than a purebred Rott, and more easily approached by strangers. Like the Lab, it may have a penchant for fetching and swimming, and be more easily trained than the dominant, stubborn Rott. But it will definitely have a more "guarded" edge to it in comparison to a Lab. None of this is written in stone though; I guess that's what makes it fun.

When considering a mixed-breed dog, first try to locate the dog's parents. If they are not available, ask about the dog's history, but take what is said with a grain or two, as they may either be guessing or holding back information. Pit bull crosses, for example, are often not identified as such because of the breed's infamous reputation, and will often be referred to as a "Lab/terrier cross," "Mastiff/retriever," or "Lab/Boxer."

Look the dog over closely. Size is a good indicator, though with puppies it can be hard to define how large the dog will grow. Puppies with big paws, thick legs and proportionally thick bodies often become big dogs. If the dog is six months old or older, you'll have a good idea about how big the dog will get, as 60 to 80 percent of its growth has already taken place.

The coat is a good clue to its lineage. A larger dog with a long, thick coat and dense undercoat often points to German Shepherd roots, but can also suggest an arctic breed such as a Husky, Malamute or Samoyed, or even a Chow Chow or Rough Collie. A short coat with no undercoat can point to a Boxer, Pit Bull, Mastiff or Pointer mix, or perhaps a sighthound hybrid. Non-shedding wiry coats often mean terrier or Poodle, or even some type of water spaniel.

Coat color helps immensely. An all-white, long, dense coat usually points to a Samoyed or American Eskimo Dog mix, whereas short white coats with dark spots often hint at a Dalmatian or Great Dane mix. Large, fawn-colored dogs with medium-to-long shedding coats often mean a Shepherd or Golden Retriever mix, while dogs with short black coats often have Lab roots.

Look closely at the dog's overall shape. Is it long and thin, like a Greyhound? Does it have a long wolfish muzzle like a Shepherd, Borzoi or Collie? Long legs, or short ones like a Dachshund or Corgi?

It's fun to reason out what breeds a mutt consists of. Just realize that it's not an exact science, and that at some point you'll need to accept whatever approximation you come up with.

Gender

The sex of the dog you choose can affect the social dynamics of the household. Male dogs in general are a bit larger than females of their own breed, and will be a tad more likely to challenge your authority at some point. They are more likely to roam and mark (even if neutered), and have a slightly higher incidence of aggression, especially toward other dogs. Males learn a bit faster though, and often have more confidence in social situations. Females are smaller, roam and mark less, and are usually (but not always) less likely to challenge your authority. They tend to be a bit more reserved, and may take longer to accept strangers. This is not a hard, fast rule; in most cases the behavioral differences between the genders is barely noticeable.

Gender becomes more of an issue in a two-dog family. In general, it is much better to alternate gender. In other words, if your current dog is male and you want a new pup, consider a female over another male. The reason? With two males in the home, there will inevitably be a struggle for dominance. Though a male and female can have the same struggle, it will not be as pronounced as the male-on-male situation.

Two males in the home are also more likely to incite each other to aggression toward a stranger or strange dog than would a male and female. This is a prime cause of dog attacks on people; if two male pit bulls or Rottweilers in a yard see a child squeezing in through the fence to get his ball back, their territorial instincts feed off of each other and create a potentially dangerous situation. With a male and female there, the danger still exists, albeit with less of a competitive, masculine zeal.

Interestingly, the same goes for females. Some of the worst dogfights I have seen took place between two females, often battling with more violent intent than two males, who usually back off once dominance is established. So, if you have a female at home, opt for a male puppy. Natural dog owners instinctively understand these gender rules, and now you do, too.

Where to Find Your Perfect Dog

The natural dog owner is not only a good judge of dogs, but a fine judge of people as well. It follows that anyone who can assume the straightforward, perceptive powers of a dog would be able to judge a person's true motivations.

There are good and bad breeders, shelters, and private owners. The good ones have the interest of the dogs at heart; the bad ones are either after pure profit, or trying to rid themselves of imperfect pets. To choose a great dog, you'll need to separate the hucksters from the dog lovers. Here's how a "natural" would find the right dog:

Breeder Selection Tips

Take your time when searching for a reputable breeder. Get references from friends, and ask local veterinarians, trainers, groomers or trusted pet care facilities. Check with established breed organizations, which will often endorse breeders in your area.

Visit numerous breeder facilities before selecting a dog. A "natural" breeder will not have profit as his or her primary motivation, but rather the future of the breed. He or she won't have too many breeding dogs on hand, and will keep the facilities hospital clean. If the place is a stinky mess, leave!

Only consider breeders you like. First impressions are always correct!

A breeder's puppies and adult dogs should all have regular access to the home, and will not always be confined to cages or crates in the garage or back property. All the dogs should receive plenty of socialization with people, and will learn house manners early on.

Caring breeders will be selective about whom they sell a dog to. If they don't ask probing questions, they aren't worth your time.

No good breeder will let a puppy go before its seventh week. If they are willing to do so, move on!

A good breeder will provide you with a health guarantee, and will require you to sign a contract. In it, you will need to promise to have your dog neutered by a certain age (if it is not a show-quality animal). If the dog is show-quality, the contract may stipulate that the breeder alone has the right to breed the dog. If a breeder offers no contract, move on.

Responsible breeders will show you all pertinent pedigree papers and vaccination records. They should also provide you with a certification of healthy hips from the OFA (Orthopedic Foundation for Animals),

BVA (British Veterinary Association) or another qualified organization.

A good breeder will ask a fair price for one of their dogs. If the price seems too good to be true, it is. Determine this fair price by comparison-shopping only with other established breeders, not newspaper classifieds.

If the breeding facility turns out to be a "backyard" operation, get back in your car. Backyard breeders are the bane of the breeding world, as they produce poor-quality puppies that pollute the gene pool and ruin the breed's reputation. Stay away from them! Avoid breeders who advertise in the classifieds, as they are usually backyard breeders looking for a quick profit, or persons looking to unload a bad dog.

Shelter Selection Tips

Reputable dog shelters adopt out millions of dogs every year. Be they purebred or mixed, these dogs usually find good homes, thanks to the work of devoted employees and volunteers. To find a good one, follow these tips:

- **Favor non-profit shelters over for-profit ones.**

- **Consider well-funded municipal facilities over underfunded locations, as they will often be able to better care for the animals. Municipal shelters will often keep dogs for a limited period of time only, however, and will euthanize dogs that do not find homes in time. That reason alone often convinces potential owners to look at municipal shelters first.**

- **Well-known private shelters with adequate funding can also be a great option. Unlike government shelters, they usually have a "no-kill" policy in effect.**

- **Visit numerous shelters before making a decision. Don't adopt out of pity, or because of a child's pleas. In fact, consider narrowing down the selection to one or two dogs before bringing your children along.**

- Choose a shelter that is clean and well run. The dogs should appear healthy, and be receiving decent food and attention as well as veterinary care when needed. All necessary vaccinations should be provided and documented.

- Choose a shelter that either neuters, or provides a certificate for future neutering. Most now neuter their dogs before they leave the premises.

- Choose a shelter that keeps careful records of the dogs on hand, including available behavioral or medical information, as well as the pet's history and training.

- Select a shelter that puts two or three dogs together, instead of keeping them alone. When shelter dogs are housed together, it means they are sociable with other dogs. Those kept singly might have antisocial issues.

When to Neuter

Most responsible owners should have their dogs neutered, in order to prevent a surplus of dogs and to minimize unwanted behaviors such as aggression, marking and roaming. But exactly when should it be done? Recently, the timing of neutering (spay for the female, castration for the male) has become an issue of contention. Standard practice in many shelters today is to neuter puppies as young as eight weeks of age, as a means of preventing unwanted births later on. Though proponents of this procedure have the best of intentions, a growing number of research veterinarians now suspect that premature neutering can adversely affect both physiological and cognitive growth in dogs.

Reproductive hormones do not just affect the development of reproductive systems in the body; in fact they regulate the development of many non-reproductive systems, including the brain, musculoskeletal system, central nervous system, vascular system, and others. Without the regulatory effects of sex hormones, these systems often do not develop fully, or in some cases (as in leg bone growth) can actually overdevelop.

My special concern has been the effects of early neutering on cognitive development. For a decade now, I have noticed that dogs neutered at a very early age have a higher incidence of slow learning and poor focus. Though only an anecdotal observation, it has recently been supported by research done at several leading veterinary colleges. Mammalian brain development appears to rely somewhat on the presence of reproductive hormones; remove them too early and the dog's future "IQ" may suffer.

My own recommendation to clients is to have female dogs neutered at six to eight months of age, at or about the time of their first estrus; and, in the case of males, any time after six months and before one year. This will allow for maximum cognitive and physiological development, both vital to training.

If your dog was neutered during puppyhood, though, don't fret. The effects of an early neuter will hardly be noticed if you follow the Seven Secrets, and do all you can to enrich and teach.

Many shelters today will not allow you to adopt a puppy until it has been neutered. Some, though, will allow you to "pre-pay" for a neuter, requiring you to get it done by the time a dog is five or six months old. If you can find a shelter willing to agree to this, go for it. This "pre-pay" agreement is often offered to those adopting females, as the spay procedure can be a bit tougher on ten-week-old puppies than can castration.

A simple compromise for ensuring both cognitive development and population control would be for veterinarians to perform tubal ligations or vasectomies on young dogs, followed up at six or eight months by neutering. This would allow for the beneficial regulatory effects of reproductive hormones on non-reproductive systems, while still ensuring that no unwanted puppies are born. Unfortunately, these procedures are expensive, and not yet widely practiced by veterinarians. Perhaps, in light of current research, they might begin to consider this option.

Pet Shops

Retail pet shops do a good job of selling pet supplies, as well as small pets such as birds, hamsters, fish and reptiles. But they strike out miserably when it comes to selling quality canines. Puppies sold in pet shops invariably come from puppy mill breeding facilities, which breed thousands of low-quality puppies each year, with the sole objective of making a profit. The bitches used to produce these inferior puppies are bred over and over until exhausted; the puppies are then sent out to thousands of pet shops that prey upon the vulnerability of well-meaning impulse buyers.

Pet shop puppies are invariably flawed in some way. Some have profound medical problems such as chronic allergies, heart disease, or hip dysplasia, while others end up as behavioral nightmares. You will never get to see a pet shop puppy's mother and father, as they are too busy breeding back at the puppy mill.

Pet shop puppies are routinely separated from their littermates at too young an age, causing profound antisocial behavior. To make matters worse, they often sit in the pet shop for months awaiting an owner, during which time no housetraining or basic obedience skills are learned. Once home, they often wreak havoc for all. In short, a natural dog owner never considers buying a dog from a pet shop.

The only exception to this rule is when a pet shop sponsors a local shelter's efforts to adopt out pets, and agrees to temporarily display dogs that are normally housed at the shelter. This allows broader access to the public and a better chance at finding a good home for a needy, healthy pet.

Testing Prospective Puppies

Once you decide on a breed-type and find a good breeding facility or shelter, you'll have to select a pet. All those cute, needy faces and wagging tails make it a daunting task, but, being a natural, you'll resist the emotional draw long enough to make an enlightened decision. Right?

The following is a reasonable procedure for selecting a puppy:

- **Choose a gender according to the previous section's advice. However, don't make this a hard, fast rule if you currently have no other dogs at home.**

- **Watch the prospective pup interact with other dogs. If it bullies the others incessantly or hides in the corner, avoid it. In general, avoid extremes in favor of a puppy that acts in a confident yet reasonable manner toward its kennel mates. Avoid lethargic puppies, as they might be ill. Also, never choose a puppy that has not socialized with others its own age, as it will have poor social skills later in life. And never consider taking a puppy before its seventh week of age, as it will not yet have had the proper littermate socialization.**

- **Now interact with the puppies. Avoid those that don't show a healthy curiosity toward you, as well as those that bite, growl, bark or challenge you. Favor a puppy that is eager to interact in a friendly manner, without being too bossy or frenetic.**

- **Look the desirable puppies over carefully, and avoid any displaying profound physical defects, discharges (from the eyes, ears, anus or reproductive organs) or infestation. Also, observe any feces present in the kennel for worms.**

Now it's time to do a quick temperament test:

- Hold each perspective puppy up so its legs are all off the
  floor. A normal puppy will struggle a bit then settle down.
  A dominant, pushy pup will continue to struggle, and may
  bite or howl. A submissive pup will dangle there passively,
  and might even submissively urinate.

- Now hold the puppy in your lap on its back. A normal
  puppy will struggle a bit then settle down, especially if you
  rub its belly. A dominant pup will struggle and whine, and
  may bite. A submissive pup will lie there passively, or may
  submissively urinate.

- Now set the puppy on the floor and toss a crumpled wad of
  paper. A normal puppy will chase it and perhaps bring it
  back when you call to it. You'll also be able to take it away.
  A dominant puppy will grab the paper and play with it,
  then ignore you when you call to it. It may also growl or
  try to bite when you take back the paper wad. A submissive
  puppy will show little interest in the paper wad, or may
  retrieve it carefully, then roll over, exposing its belly.

Select the "normal," or middle-of-the-road puppy. Doing so will
almost always result in a reasonable, cooperative pet.

Testing an Older Dog

The same basic rules apply to choosing an older dog, except you
won't be lifting it up off the floor. You should look for any abnormal
physical or behavioral characteristics, and avoid any dogs that display
overt aggression or fear. Take a pass on dogs that show overly pushy,
dominant behavior, in favor of one that finds you an interesting distraction. Calmness and a desire to be handled are big plusses, as is decent
focus. Pass on any dog that is being kept by itself, as this often hints at

antisocial behavior. The exception to this is if the dog is recovering from illness.

After observing an adult dog with other dogs, be sure to clip a leash on it and take it for a walk around the shelter grounds. If they do not permit this, seek out another shelter. You have to get a feel for what the dog is like outside of the kennel environment; walking it around will do a good job of that. When you do, ask it to sit, to see if it has had any obedience training. Odds are any dog over six months of age will have had some.

When adopting an older dog, most people opt for one under a year in age. This usually works out well; the dog is old enough for you to determine its true size and character, yet young enough to still have it's behavior and personality molded by you. Plus, you can be assured of many years of fun and good health.

Don't ignore the benefits of adopting an older dog. An adult pet often has excellent housetraining skills, and enough basic obedience training to make the transition to your world easy. They are normally calmer and more focused, and have a well-established personality. Be aware, however, that mature shelter dogs are sometimes given up by their owners because of medical conditions requiring regular veterinary care. Also, a mature dog may not get along with children or with any established pets you have in the home. If you do fall for an older dog, rule out any medical problems, and make sure it likes your children. If allowed by the shelter, let it meet and interact with any dog you currently own, to insure they socialize well.

Using Your Current Dog's History and Heredity to Your Benefit

For most of you, the choice of dog has already occurred. The issue of choosing wisely will therefore come into play only when selecting an additional or replacement pet. But a true "natural" owner learns as much as possible about his or her current canine friend's heredity and history to better understand its unique needs and tendencies. Doing so helps optimize the set-up of the home environment, and focus attention on do's and don'ts particular to a dog's breed-specific type. If you aspire to be a natural owner, you'll do the same.

For instance, if you own a Weimaraner, know that it is a tireless breed with a remarkable sense of smell, and an initial wariness toward strangers. You'll need to exercise it daily, obedience train it to overcome the distraction of its nose, and socialize it often with people and other dogs. *Don't* expect a Weimaraner to be happy inside an apartment all day.

Have a Papillon? These lively, diminutive toys get along fabulously with children, but can easily injure their delicate legs. Accordingly, kids in the home must be taught not to roughhouse with the dog, or encourage it to jump down from tables or chairs.

Soft-coated Wheaten Terrier? Gentler and more demure than other terriers, they require a soft hand at training, and patient, brief training sessions with positive reinforcement. If you've been a bit hard on yours, ease up, but avoid comforting the dog when it shows fear or confusion.

Whatever the breed, learn all you can, then apply what you've learned to your attitude and home environment. Take your Lab for a swim; run your Greyhound more; take your Border Collie to agility class—whatever the breed needs to express its natural tendencies. *Be the dog*—know what it craves!

If you have a mixed breed, do the same kind of breed research, then apply what you've learned to your pet. For example, if your dog is a Shepherd/Lab cross, expect it to be an active, intelligent pet with the need for regular exercise and grooming. It will require early socialization and obedience training (due to the Shepherd side), and will love to swim or retrieve a ball all day long (the Lab side).

A Pug/Beagle (or "Puggle") mix? Expect a happy, active little dog with a penchant for barking (Beagle) and snorting (Pug). It will have a low-maintenance coat (both breeds), and be distracted by scent (Beagle), requiring early and consistent training, especially with the recall or "Come Here" command. It may experience sinus infections and eye irritations (Pug), and put on weight easily (both breeds).

After reviewing the section entitled *"Choosing a Mixed Breed,"* delve into your dog's genetic background and apply what you learn to your own behavior and environment. In this way, you will come to know your canine friend in the same way you would a friend from a different culture.

Don't neglect your dog's specific history. For instance, if your pet experienced abuse at the hands of children early on, know that it may show suspicion toward them for it's entire life. To modify this, you could have well-mannered, mature kids feed your dog, take it for walks, or play "Fetch" with it.

If your dog has a history of digging beneath a fence and getting out, be sure to modify the fence in such a way as to prevent this from happening again. A concrete runner or a line of chicken wire buried beneath the fence will usually do nicely. Does the dog jump over fences? Raising the fence height or building a dog pen will usually dissuade the dog from this behavior.

Was your dog in a shelter for a long period? Shelter dogs often have unreliable housetraining habits, and may exhibit separation anxiety more than others. If this is the case for your dog, consider a higher level of home supervision regarding housetraining, including possible crate feeding and training, and perhaps regular play visits with the neighbor's dog to modify separation issues.

Bad skin allergies early in life? Dogs who suffered from this often develop a habit of scratching incessantly, even when skin irritations are long gone. With these dogs, be sure to use a veterinarian-approved, preventive flea/tick medication, and avoid washing them too often, as this can cause dry skin and stimulate itching again. When washing, use the mildest soap possible, and rinse well.

Learn all you can about your dog, then apply what you learn to your relationship, to make life for both of you as meaningful as possible. Being aware of your pet's drives and experiences means you are a natural dog owner!

Understand and Apply Leadership, the Sacred Canine Code

Understanding the Wolf Pack

The wolf that argues governing systems is a dead wolf.

Canis lupus, or the grey wolf, is a superb survivor, able to thrive in nearly any ecosystem the world can throw at it. Besides its undeniable intellect and physical prowess, what is the wolf's secret to survival?

For the answer, look to our own primal beginnings. Like the wolf, early humans were intensely social creatures with a penchant for group cooperation, at least on a small, tribal scale. The survival of the collective was the goal, period; all else was incidental.

Early humans had a hierarchical control structure; the strongest, smartest, and most capable elders made decisions about where to hunt, with whom to fight or mate, or when to move the tribe. With few exceptions, this type of control lasted until the first fledgling steps toward true democracy were taken.

Wolves haven't taken that step yet, and probably never will, as their hierarchical style of governance just works too well to change. Highly social, wolves band together into small packs, each possessing a distinct pecking order. Capable leadership by the alpha male wolf keeps the peace, and insures the pack's success. The alpha female, who dominates the females, nearly always mates exclusively with the alpha male. Their litter is the only one produced each season; the rest of the pack dutifully helps nurture them in every way, just as a large, loving family might.

Unlike cats, wolves typically hunt prey larger than themselves. This requires a great degree of tactical cooperation between pack members. This need for teamwork helped the wolf develop a healthy social dynamic, a vital component of intelligence. To hold this tactical relationship together, wolves opted for a hierarchical social structure.

People often mistakenly think this hierarchical arrangement to be severe, and egocentric by nature. The opposite in fact is true. Few animals show the loyalty, allegiance and affection that wolves do. The leader, rather than being dictatorial and selfish, shows great restraint, especially toward juveniles in the pack, who get to "mix it up" with other juveniles so as to establish their own eventual pack status. The alpha male rarely punishes, and never flaunts his vaunted position by stealing a submissive wolf's food ration. He is intrinsically fair-minded and patient, and lets his wolves get away with much provided it doesn't undermine his control or the pack's safety.

The alpha is more of a revered elder than a feared general. The leader *motivates* and *inspires* the pack to perform by setting an example, as would a respected role model in our society. This is the embodiment of the *natural* method.

It is important to understand that the alpha wolf attains his position not just through physical and psychological dominance, but through his popularity and ability to lead. The others *want* to follow him because he makes them feel safe, confident, and important. He does not coerce them, but instead leads by example. Nothing artificial about it; the alpha's "cult of personality" creates harmony in the pack.

In exchange for leadership, the alpha demands some tribute. He has the privilege of siring the pack's litters, until too old to dissuade his competitors. This ensures that ensuing pups will carry the pack's most capable genes, increasing future pack success.

When directly involved in stalking, chasing and killing prey, the alpha usually gets first access to the kill, though he certainly does not prevent others from feeding. He chooses a prime sleeping spot, often an elevated place from where he can see his pack. He dominates whatever space he happens to be in. He initiates contact with outsiders, leads the pack on long marches, and disciplines when necessary. For as long as he can maintain control, he is basically the "big daddy."

If a wolf went against the pack dynamic, he or she would most likely be rejected by the rest of the pack, and end up alone. Lone wolves do poorly in the wild; without another pack willing to take them in, they often die. Such is the price to pay for disrespecting the old ways.

The Canine Craving

The same pack instincts present in wolves are found in domestic canines. Be it a Malamute or Maltese, the desire to be part of a successful group is the single most compelling force in a dog's life. They crave structure and leadership as much as companionship and affection. In fact, love between dogs and their owners is *inextricably linked to pack position and aspiration*; the dog that accepts a subordinate place will always show more "affection" to confident, dominant humans.

Leadership is the lifeblood of the dog; without it they, like the lone wolf, lose touch with their heritage and become disconnected from the natural order of things. And that's when behavior troubles begin.

In a perfect world, your dog's social status should be below that of the humans in its "pack." The dog should look to you and your family for guidance while being instinctively obedient, just as wolves of low rank are to the alpha leader.

Unfortunately, this is often not the case. By denying the dog's need to be led, many owners inadvertently force their pets to become the leaders of their own "packs," spawning all manner of behavioral problems. Without a leader to look up to, your dog must take charge; this results in pushy, controlling, or even aggressive behavior.

More happens inside your dog's mind and heart than love, loyalty and a need to eat and play. Your dog is always seeking to clarify and improve its position in the "pack" hierarchy. If its position in the pack is unclear, or if the top spot appears vacant, *it will aspire to rise up in the pecking order*. Without a demonstrative role model (read natural owner), your dog will be compelled to take on the role of alpha.

Canines become troubled by a passive provider who mistakenly thinks he or she is actually in charge. If you inadvertently portray yourself as a passive subordinate, your dog will have no choice but to attempt bloodless coups d'etat, regardless of its inherent level of dominance. Make no mistake; it has no choice. They need to know someone competent is calling the shots, and hate to ask: "*Who's running the show?*"

Leaderless

Leadership is the magic social bond for all canines. It's not a machination of authoritarian control freaks; it's real, and it colors most of a dog's actions. Unfortunately, many owners don't understand this.

When a dog cannot identify a leader, it attempts to assume that role itself because it simply cannot live in a pack without one. Like the sole surviving Marine in a decimated platoon, the dog takes over operations despite having little command experience. Often the owner does not even see it coming, at least not in the beginning when the problem is still manageable.

Most times the owner of a dominant dog will eventually begin to rationalize his or her dog's antisocial behavior, telling guests that "*he got scared by the postal carrier and hates people now,*" or "*she doesn't like tall people,*" or "*he'll only eat when we feed him from the table.*" They actually become quite skilled at denying or masking problems.

Soon they are forced to isolate the dog from others to avoid conflict and embarrassment. This is an *unnatural* solution; eventually the symptoms of a leaderless, dominant dog make life harder and harder for its owner, and for the dog too.

These dogs lose much of their social, accepting nature, and gradually become pushy, cranky, neurotic and controlling. Most soon resort to overt disobedience, growling or even biting to reinforce their new positions of authority. Some dogs handle the new position easily, while others less capable become nervous little time bombs.

Why They Take Over

When a dog is pampered like a surrogate child, humanization occurs. The owner treats the pet as an equal; unfortunately, this parity is perceived by the dog not as a democratic ideal but as *acquiescence of its dominance*. Remember; in a dog's mind, equality is a free pass to the top.

The canine brain is wired differently than ours. We have a dissimilar biological heritage, and divergent behavioral drives. One cannot simply assign human qualities to an animal, no matter how endearing or intelligent that animal may seem.

Nevertheless, it's done every day; owners give their dogs the freedom to choose, the freedom to come and go, the freedom to eat when and what they want, the right to sleep in a human bed—in short, they teach the dog that it has all the powers of the alpha.

A humanized dog gets unearned praise and attention, status and privilege. It is made the center of attention, and is allowed to initiate behaviors. If it wants to be petted, the humanized, dominant dog shoves its head onto a human lap, demanding a pet (which it gets). It regularly assumes a dominant position, normally on the owner's lap, chair or bed. It receives minimal training, creating a poor response factor. It gets no consistent human response and is rarely disciplined, partly due to its aggressive response to any attempts by the owner to feign authority.

A humanized, dominant dog controls space and possessions, and more or less sets its own daily agenda, ignoring its owner's requests. It disciplines the other pack members (as is its right) through growling or biting, pulls incessantly on leash, and sleeps in its owner's bed (or the bed of a child). It regularly plays strength games such as wrestling or tug-of-war with its owner, which teach it that it can vie with the humans for physical dominance. It also plays chase games with adults and children, which it always wins. This confirms the dog's physical superiority over all people, another reinforcement of its dominance.

Slowly, the barrage of attention and privilege convinces the dog that it is the boss (whether or not it wants to be). When a dog becomes the leader of its pack, it:

- **Gains the authority to act independently**

- **Has the right and responsibility to discipline others in its group, including humans**

- **Can ignore "subordinates"**

- **Presumes it owns everything, and has dominion over all pack activity**

- **Can monitor and control comings and goings of housemates and guests**

- **Protects food, desired sleeping areas, possessions and schedules**

- **Develops heightened territorial instincts**

- **Is less likely to socialize with friends and strangers**

These behaviors are often interpreted by coddling owners as disobedience or aggression, when in fact the dog is simply *acting normally*, according to its ascension to the leadership throne. This is the biggest cause of disobedience and dog bites, as well as the abandonment or euthanization of dogs. The coddling owner doesn't understand that, if you inadvertently hand the keys to the castle to a dog, it will take them, and play "keep-away" for as long as it can.

Why You Should Embrace the Canine Perspective of Leadership

Picture a child with parents who allow any behavior, no matter how dangerous or absurd. Though a tempting prospect to any precocious, independent-minded youngster, it would quickly degrade into a dangerous, daunting situation. Without the umbrella of parental protection and authority, children become apprehensive and uncertain about inter-actions with the outside world. They crave role models and guidance, especially at an early age, in order to develop the confidence and autonomy needed to tackle the world at large later on.

Dogs are even more reliant on guidance and leadership. They literally cannot function normally without these, and sink into an unbalanced "free-for-all" mindset when denied a sense of social order and loyalty. The dominant dog denied leadership becomes belligerent and officious, while the leaderless submissive dog becomes neurotic and indignant over having to take over administration of the pack. This is the exclusive purview of the coddler, and the engine of creation for dysfunctional dogs everywhere.

It needn't be that way. By becoming a proxy alpha dog and embracing the canine perspective of loving leadership, you will set the stage for a happy, confident dog/owner relationship, one which rewards the owner with respect, reliability and devotion, and the dog with confidence, calmness, and the comfort of knowing that there is a creditable captain at the helm.

How to Become a Natural Leader

Establishing yourself as the benevolent leader of your pack need not be a struggle. If you have the conviction to stick with my leadership plan for three months, you will succeed in establishing (or re-establishing) your-self as the home CEO, the first (and most crucial) step in becoming a natural owner.

It all boils down to you, the lead "dog," managing your dog's access to privileges, space, food, and interactions. That's basically it. These are the things dogs need; by properly managing your dog's access to them, you will establish yourself as the pack "executive," and gradually change your position from peer to parent in your dog's eyes.

The following are key techniques you should adopt to initiate your "rise to the top." Remember: it's as much for the well being of your dog as it is for you.

The Alpha Eats First

Unless he has not participated in the actual hunt, the alpha leader always eats first. That is a time-tested indicator of dominance and leadership; wolves that have first dibs on a kill are predictably dominant over more submissive pack members, who must wait their turn, or at best meekly move in for a bite here and there while waiting until higher-ups have sated themselves. It's not democratic; it's just the way it is. This system insures that the most important members of the pack maintain their strength and virility for hunting and mating purposes.

Wolves also use feeding time to attempt shifts in the pack hierarchy. For instance, if two juveniles possess equal status, they will often jockey for feeding rights in order to move up in rank. Fights can result; eventually the more dominant wolf wins out and leapfrogs the loser in pack status. Access to food becomes not only a nutritional necessity, it's also the mechanism to gain higher standing.

Domestic dogs do this too, often without their owners knowing. I once had a client whose geriatric Chihuahua used to teeter atop the dinner table and eat *from his owner's plate.* The dog was a holy terror to everyone including his devoted owner, who simply kept her precious little biting buzz saw away from people, to prevent injury.

The owner chose to feed her dog in this way because she considered the dog her equal, and because she liked the company at dinnertime. The dog truly had become a surrogate mate to her, a strange little canine chauvinist whose leadership status demanded he eat whatever he wanted, whenever, and wherever. Needless to say, the owner was a submissive coddler.

Most owners are not this nutty about their dogs. Nevertheless, the majority feed their dogs improperly, and in doing so teach them to be dominant. For example: those of you who come home from work and feed your dogs right away, before eating yourselves, are telling your dogs they have higher status. Like an alpha wolf, they eat first, and derive from this a sense of superiority. And when they see that your first act upon arriving home is to feed them, it reinforces their belief that you are a subordinate.

Those of you who free-feed your dogs are guilty as well. Free-feeding, or leaving food down all day, tells dogs that they are important enough to have a limitless supply of food, as compared to humans, who seem not to. And when food is always available, the owner loses the ability to affect the dog's behavior through the delivery of food at a precise time, for a specific reason. They become less interested in treats as well, making training more difficult.

Begging is another way for dogs to dominate their owners. Think about it: when a dog approaches a person eating and that person dutifully gives them something off his or her plate, what has happened? Simple; the dog has trained that person to surrender food whenever it wants. That's power, and dominance. Give in to this form of owner masochism and you elevate your dog even higher in the pack.

Being proxy alpha dogs, natural owners know the power of food, and manage it accordingly. You need to follow their lead and learn to manage food as a means to leadership. Once you do, your dog will understand that you are a potent, charitable leader. Here's how:

Feed your dog after you eat Before you prepare and serve your dog's meal, be sure *you eat first*. Let him know you are eating; let him watch from a distance, as do submissive wolves. If he can't control himself during your meal, place him in another room or in a dog crate. Only after you have finished eating should you prepare and serve his food. By setting this precedent and sticking to it for *the rest of your dog's life*, you will reestablish your power over food, and teach your pet that he must be *below you* in the pack.

Avoid free-feeding your dog As stated earlier, free-feeding your dog teaches him that, because food is always present, he must be superior to humans, who only have limited access to food. Also, when you free-feed, the food isn't really *coming from you*; it's just there in the bowl. You lose the ability to teach him that you hold the power of the food dish.

The alpha wolf finds the prey, kills it, then allows others to eat when he is done. That's what you should do too. So, feed your dog at specific times, either once or twice per day. And before you place the food down, make him sit for it. By making him earn the food, you reinforce your status as leader.

Make your dog earn all treats When a dog gets treats for no particular reason, it begins to develop a superior mindset, thinking that it must have great standing in the pack. Over time, this can seriously affect an owner's place in the hierarchy. Coddlers are famous for this boo-boo; the very act of their surrogate canine children eating treats from their hands makes them *feel* good, because the dog is responding to something they are doing. In reality, this is *the dog training the owner*.

Never give gratis treats; instead, make your dog do *something* first before handing out the goodies. Sit, shake, rollover, bark—any behavior at all will work. Just make him understand that he must *earn* a treat. This will help you teach him who's the leader.

Feed multiple dogs in order of dominance Remember that, in homes with multiple dogs, a dominance hierarchy exists between them, too. It's not hard to identify this; usually the dominant dog greets people first, bullies the others for treats and toys, disciplines the others when they get out of hand, and just maintains an air of authority over the others. Natural owners can instinctively identify the hierarchy, and usually even coddlers can, too.

Coddlers often make the mistake of not honoring that dog hierarchy, and instead enforcing more egalitarian, democratic rules. For instance, when giving three dogs treats, they will often neglect to hand them out according to pack status. This is insulting to the alpha dog, and can lead to fights and pack anxiety, not only for the alpha, but for the others as well. Coddlers will also chastise a dominant dog for barking or growling at a more submissive pet, even though it's exactly what they are supposed to do. The dominant dog disciplines those below him, remember?

Being proxy dogs, natural owners let the dogs work it out, unless physical harm is imminent.

Always feed your dogs in accordance to their place in the pack. The dominant dog is often the eldest animal, whose seniority lends authority until it becomes too old to maintain the position. It can sometimes be the biggest dog, though size is often not the indicator. I've seen Pomeranians lord it over Great Danes, so don't assume size alone is the deciding factor.

If you watch them closely, the pecking order should become obvious. The alpha dog will demand attention from you first, and will usually greet or confront strangers before the others do, and will lead the others when moving from one area to another. So, when placing food bowls down, do so in order of dominance. Do the same when handing out treats, making sure that all the dogs earn these. If your dogs show aggression toward each other at feeding time, feed them separately, to prevent injury.

The Alpha Goes First

The leader of a pack goes first because he is best qualified to do so. He confronts strange wolves, tracks and kills prey, evaluates potential dangers, and determines in which direction the pack should travel. With the most experience, the alpha gets the call to lead the troops.

The responsibility of going first translates into status. When the others see him out ahead coping with whatever comes his way, they derive a sense of confidence and well being, and a strong feeling of respect for his capabilities and courage. This deference translates into unquestioned dominance for the alpha.

Coddlers don't understand the "go first" rule. They let their dogs burst in and out of doors first, and have little control over greetings with people and other dogs. They allow their dogs to pull out ahead on leash, and play chase games in which the dog always wins. When sensing danger, a coddler's dog takes charge. And a coddler's dog rarely comes when called, because it's too busy forging out ahead, doing whatever it wants.

A natural owner always initiates contact with strangers and strange dogs. He or she decides where to go on a walk, what to do if danger lurks, when to come home, where to let his or her dogs relieve themselves. The natural goes in and out of doors first, and does not let a dog mindlessly pull ahead on leash. The natural never chases his or her dog, instead opting to have the dog do the chasing. And a natural never has trouble getting his or her dog to come when called because, when the boss calls, something must be afoot. By taking the lead both physically and emotionally, the natural sets an example for his or her dog, and solidifies his or her leadership status.

The Alpha Leader goes through doors first The natural dog owner takes care never to let his or her dog rush through a door first for several reasons. First, it is a sign of weakness to let your dog blow by you, going out or in. If you are in charge, it is your privilege and responsibility to go first, in case something dangerous lurks on the other side. Dogs that rush by their coddling owners dismiss whatever leadership the person thinks he or she has, and reinforce their own ideas of autonomy. Plus, they often find trouble on the other side; disrespectful dogs who rush out doors often get into fights with other dogs, get hit by cars, or at the very least run off and get lost, or jump all over arriving guests. Rushing through an open door also shows that the dog is not thinking but simply reacting to stimuli, a true sign of a coddled, mentally under-stimulated dog. Teaching a dog to wait for a moment gets his brain engaged, a key factor in natural dog ownership.

The "wait at the door" command helps put the brakes on this by teaching the dog to think about boundaries and manners. Use it coming in and out of the home, at curbs, and even in the home when your dog needs a lesson or two in obedience.

Here's how to teach your dog to wait at a door while you first go through:

- Place a bright strip of tape down at the open entrance to a room in your home.

- With your dog on a six-foot leash, lead him up to the boundary.

- Have him sit, then say "Wait." Give the verbal command and a hand sign, a palm in his face.

- Step through sideways while holding the leash in such a way as to prevent him from following you through. Stand directly in front of him if necessary to prevent him from stepping over the line. If he is particularly difficult, have a helper hold the leash to stop him from rushing through.

- If he still tries to sneak through, correct with a quick pop of the leash toward the inside of the home, while simultaneously saying "No, Wait." When he does wait, even for a moment, praise.

- Work this until you can step through without the dog following. Praise him when he begins to get the idea. When ready for the dog to follow you through, say "Okay!" and call the dog through. Praise and reward with a treat when he succeeds.

- Gradually increase the distance between you and the dog, and the time he waits. Once mastered inside the home, try it at the front and back doors, and at curbs. Eventually you should be able to drop the leash, walk away, and have the dog wait until the "Okay" is given. Wean him off treats in favor of praise, with an infrequent treat used as reinforcement.

Mastering this exercise gives you a great tool in reigning in your dog's impetuous nature and in establishing your dominance, an essential factor in becoming a natural owner. You can even adapt the "Wait" command to a spot in the home, say a small rug or even an open crate; having your dog temporarily wait at a specific location like this can help calm the dog down, especially at your dinnertime, or when guests come by.

The Alpha Leader walks a dog on a loose leash The most common misbehavior by dogs has to be pulling out ahead on leash. It is so common, in fact, that most owners think it a normal behavior. The reverse is true; when a dog forges out ahead of its owner while on leash, it leads the parade and assumes control. By allowing this, coddlers surrender leadership and position to their dogs. They unintentionally ask their pets to take over all aspects of the walk, including direction and speed, when and where to eliminate, or who to interact with along the way. The dog literally walks the owner.

Even more telling is the mindset created by allowing a dog to pull out ahead on leash. When a dog does so, he stops thinking about his owner completely and goes into reactionary mode, instead of thinking clearly about what's going on. When the leash is taut, the dog knows exactly where his owner is, and need not pay attention to human input anymore. He can simply forge out ahead like a sled dog and forget about the subordinate coddler being dragged along behind.

Leash tension can also be a signal to a dog that his owner is worried about something, perhaps a stray dog or a group of persons approaching. When confronted with a possible concern, the coddler will often tighten up on the leash; the dog interprets this as fear, the last thing a leader should project when confronted. It makes the dog feel insecure, and can lead to canine fear aggression and a loss of status for the owner. This is one reason why dogs are so much more likely to get into fights when on the end of a tight leash, as opposed to running free.

Walking your dog on a loose leash forces him to pay attention to you, something dominant dogs rarely do with coddling owners. Ironic when one considers that, above all else, the coddler craves his or her dog's attention. The exact opposite actually occurs; like a teenager who thinks his parents are dorks, the dog of a coddler often completely ignores his owner whenever outdoors.

The dog of a natural owner enjoys walking just as much as the next dog, but with one key difference. It considers the walk a shared pack experience, and will often look to its owner for approval, opinion or direction during the process, just as subordinates in a wolf pack defer to the alpha when necessary. They too are on "loose leashes" of sorts, leashes made not of leather or cloth, but of allegiance and obligation. The natural dog owner knows that the leash is there simply to correct if necessary, or to prevent calamity from occurring.

Before describing how to train your dog to walk on a loose leash, I want to say a word about spring-loaded, retractable leashes. Used by many, they can be an excellent way to allow a trained, respectful dog to wander off as far as twenty feet, to explore or relieve itself, without actually having to be let off-leash. And they can be an invaluable aid in teaching a reliable recall, one of the harder commands to master. But coddlers often opt for this type of leash from the start without first training their dogs to walk civilly on a normal six-foot leash. The result is a dog that can ignore its owner to an even greater degree than one pulling out on the end of a six-foot leash. Retractable leashes have compounded the problem of disrespectful, disobedient dogs by reinforcing the idea that a dog needn't pay any attention at all to its owner. So, before using a retractable leash, always first train your dog to walk on the loose, six-foot variety.

Before teaching your dog to walk on a loose leash, you'll need to decide between two different equipment options regarding the type of collar used. When I train, I normally choose a traditional "slip" collar (incorrectly referred to as a choke chain). When used properly this age-old tool works quite well, and causes no actual pain or damage to a dog's throat. Rather, it tightens uniformly and quickly around the dog's neck whenever the owner/trainer administers a fast "pop" on the leash. This "correction" is not given as a punishment, but rather as a wake-up call to the dog, a way of saying "*you aren't doing it right, pal; pay closer atten-tion*." In conjunction with the "pop" is the sound the chain collar makes when a correction is properly given—a zippy, ratcheting sound that becomes a signal to the dog, an audible way of saying "nope" to the pet. Again, it is not supposed to cause physical pain; if it does, you aren't doing it right.

For this exercise, however, I'm going to recommend you use what is called a "face" collar. Sold under numerous brand names, it fits over the dog's muzzle and has a "D" ring attachment for the leash that hangs down below the pet's lower jaw. Operating like a bridle on a horse (without the bit), it makes controlling a pulling dog easy, even for kids. The operating principle is that if you control the head, you control the animal.

Go to your local pet store and have the clerk help you fit a properly-sized face collar to your dog. Then, before even using it on walks, get your pooch acclimated to it by having him wear it for increasingly long periods of time in the home. It will take some getting used to; at first he may try to rub it off his face with a paw. Try rewarding him with cookies each time you put it on him, and while he has it on. Start out with a minute, then over a few days time extend that to an hour or two. Just be positive and sure of yourself. And once you decide to do it, do not allow the dog to decide otherwise.

Once you have your dog desensitized to the face collar, it's time to clip a leash on and start training him to walk by your side in a calm, controlled fashion. Here's how:

- **Start first around the home, without distraction. Clip the leash onto the "D" ring hanging below his mouth and start moving slowly around the home, changing direction ran-domly. Lure him around with a treat if need be. When he feels any pressure on the face collar, he will turn his head in the direction of that pressure, just as a horse would.**

- **Take a confident, stoic attitude at first, as he may object to the "imposition." Just require him to follow your lead. When** he does begin to walk nicely around the home, give him a treat or two as a reward. You will quickly begin to understand the benefits of using the face collar; it requires little leash tension, and causes absolutely no physical discomfort for the dog.

- Keep your leash as loose as possible during this trial home walk; use a happy disposition and positive encouragement to get him moving nicely. You can even entice him with a piece of chicken if needed; just get him moving on a loose leash with you changing direction and speed.

- Soon he will understand that you are directing the show. Keep him right by your left side, his shoulders even with your body. Changing directions unpredictably will force him to pay attention to you, so do it often. Turn in front of him to your left; stop suddenly, and vary your pace. The face collar will make it impossible for even the most pushy dog to determine direction, so be confident, positive and authoritative. After five minutes of this, remove the face collar, praise and reward him, then have break.

- After a few days of indoor training with no distractions, it's time to take the show outside. Choose a backyard if available, again with as few distractions as possible. Repeat the same techniques used in the home, only with more verve, speed and directional changes. He'll be more apt to try to resist when outside, so be on your toes; keep treats handy for enticement purposes, and consider limiting the session to only a few minutes at a time. Remember; keep your leash loose at all times unless the need to direct the dog becomes necessary. Soon you will notice your dog responding to your position, and adjusting his motions accordingly. That's the start of respect, and focus.

- Once he'll walk nicely by your side, take him for a walk down a quiet street, again changing direction often, to improve his ability to respond to your directional changes. Reverse direction; make full circles in both directions; stop suddenly—whatever it takes to get him to pay attention to you. Move quickly, with confidence.

- Over a period of a week or two, gradually introduce distractions into the mix. Walk him down a busy street; have kids walk by; take him past a yard with barking dogs—whatever it takes to test his focus. Be on your toes, and settle for nothing less than his acceptance of your directional authority. Remember that it is your walk, not his; once he accepts this, the experience will be much more pleasing to both of you.

- After eight to ten weeks of walking your dog on a face collar, try walking him on a regular collar instead, to see if he has learned to focus. Leave the face collar on at first; just clip to his regular collar instead. With the face collar still on, he'll think the same conditions apply. If you've done your job, he'll walk nicely for you.

Eventually you'll be able to remove the face collar and walk him on a normal collar, without any pulling. Return to the face collar if he shows any backsliding, though; give it a few days, then try the regular collar again. It's a learning process for both of you, so be patient and committed. Soon, you will accomplish this first great step in readjusting the leadership hierarchy; you will be in charge of the walk, and he will begin focusing on you, and on the bond between you.

The Alpha Leader never chases his or her dogs In the wolf pack, you'll be hard-pressed to find an alpha male or female chasing after a submissive wolf, unless it is to catch and discipline the rascal. When they do so, however, rest assured that they will catch the character quickly.

In the wild world, the contrary is more likely; the subordinate wolves often chase after the more dominant animals, either while hunting or in play. This reinforces the pecking order, maintaining pack stability.

Unfortunately, humans are as slow as molasses compared to dogs. Even little dogs are often faster than us two-foots; it's simply a function of legs and proportional muscle power. As far as chase games go, humans will lose nearly every time.

Why is this significant? Simple: if you regularly chase after your dog and always lose the race, he will soon understand that he is faster and more agile than you. Speed and agility are attributes of dominance; he will begin to think of you as a subordinate.

When this happens, he will start playful little keep-away games with you, and may begin disobeying direct commands in favor of goading you into a game you cannot win. It's play, but it's serious too. Play among dogs is *always* related to pack positioning; if you lose, you sink down.

You know that your dog will win that race every time, but he doesn't until it's proven to him. So, instead of giving him the opportunity to discover his physical superiority, opt to never chase after him. Instead, from the very beginning, make him chase *you* around the yard. If he breaks off and tries to goad you into chasing him, simply run off in a different direction, turning the tables on him. He'll choose to chase you, and in the process learn that you are choreographing playtime.

The Alpha Leader asserts a dominant bearing Just recently I lost a great dog, a Rottweiler/Shepherd mix named Louie, who lived to the ancient age of sixteen years and two days, unheard of for a dog of his breed lineage. Louie had a special mix of confidence and empathy; he believed in his own relative authority over other dogs, but practiced great latitude with them, allowing them to work out the relationship provided they didn't get too physical or insulting. He was patient and tolerant almost to a fault, but knew when to draw the line and defend his honor and safety.

I often used Louie to help socialize dominant or fearful dogs and bring them back into the fold, so to speak. Louie was friendly, but knew when to lay down the law. He was sensitive but strong, and more than capable of defending himself (and me) from an aggressive dog in need of behavior modification. Louie was the perfect re-entry mechanism for these antisocial animals who, once desensitized to his presence, then became amenable to contact with other dogs and people.

Louie did it with a confident air, strength of personality, judicious restraint, physical power if need be, and the proper application of body posture at the proper time. He read other dogs' intentions better than I could, and used what he learned to determine a course of action. I learned much from Louie, and for that I am in his debt.

Dogs are masters of posturing, in both a physical and psychological sense. Watch two dogs meet for the first time and you will quickly understand; most will nose each other for a moment then go tail-to-tail, sniffing out each other's life history. In seconds they know gender, genital status (neutered or not), age, health, stress levels, hormonal activity—the works.

Then they begin a ritualistic posturing; if one dog is clearly submissive to the other, it takes on a placid countenance, with the tail tucked, ears back, and the eyes somewhat lidded. It licks at the dominant dog's mouth, and may even roll over and go belly-up, with a bit of submissive urination. The dominant dog holds himself upright, with ears perked and tail up and proud, carriage strong and confident. It may even mount the submissive dog or place its front legs atop the other's shoulders.

If the two dogs are headed for aggression, one sees hackles raise and carriage tense, with weight on the rear legs, ready to pounce or run. Lips pull back to expose fangs, and tails become tense and low. Snarls can lead to aggression, or to one dog backing off and accepting the other's dominance. A ritual played out for millions of years, it's unlikely to change.

Happy, playful dogs take a light-hearted posture, with front lowered, tail wagging and mouth open and smiling (yes they can smile). A romp often ensues; these two have little desire to get serious about the keys to the kingdom, at least not just yet.

In general, the alpha leader asserts a dominant bearing over others in his pack. His posture, eye contact, and overall demeanor is confident, almost haughty; he exudes physical and psychological competence. As the natural CEO of your home, you must be aware of posture and use it to your benefit, to reinforce your dominance and help your dog feel well governed. In general, your dog should never be allowed to use his body to gain privilege, or to alter your behavior.

The following are ways you can assert yourself, and in doing so help establish the proper pecking order in the home:

Maintain an upright posture while training and disciplining
Whenever working with your dog on basic obedience behaviors or when disciplining your dog in any way, keep yourself physically higher than your dog. To better understand this, try this experiment. Sit on the floor beside your dog and ask him to sit. Odds are he won't do it, and will instead look at you as if you're crazy. Now stand up and repeat the command; odds are he will sit quickly. It's all a matter of altitude!

The exception to this is when teaching the recall or "Come Here" command. A dog will be much more likely to come to you when you crouch down and call him happily. You become a more inviting target; the dog will be magnetically drawn to you.

Keep your dog off your furniture So many owners violate this cardinal rule that it deserves to be discussed. In a dog's mind, if it is allowed to sleep or rest at the same height (and in the same spot) as another dog, it then has equal status in the pack. Dominant pack members covet their resting spots, and will chase off underlings who usurp that space, unless it is a young pup.

Coddlers humanize their dogs, and as such desire them to rest with them in bed, chair or sofa. Without realizing it, they lend equality to their dogs, leading to behavior problems and an ambiguous understanding of the pecking order.

Every time I come across an aggressive or pushy dog, I ask if the dog sleeps in the owner's bed, and invariably get the answer "of course." Owners of toy dogs are notoriously guilty of this; they simply *must* have their furry little bundles in their bed, chair or sofa. Eventually, when others try to sit on the bed, chair or sofa, the dog becomes incensed, and will bark or bite in an attempt to evict the "invader."

To avoid this, keep your pooch off of your preferred resting areas, especially your bed. Remember, it's a dog, not a suckling infant. Regarding a chair or sofa, if your dog has dominance issues, keep him off. But, once you establish yourself as a strong effective leader, you can (if you must) allow your dog up only when you are with it, upon giving it permission. Give the command "*Up*," being sure to praise. Then give the command "*Off*." Then require the dog to get off the sofa or chair when you desire; use a leash and collar if need be. When the dog gets off, praise and reward. By making it a controllable behavior, you maintain control and authority.

If you wish to lie with your dog, move down onto the floor or carpet with him. In doing so, you'll send him the message that groupings will occur on his turf (the floor) and not up high, where humans abide. When you do so, that turf temporarily falls under your jurisdiction. You commandeer *his* turf, and not vice-versa.

In my opinion the bed should always be off-limits. And unless you bathe and brush your dog on a daily basis (a bad idea for the health of a dog's skin and coat), why would you *want* your pooch to share the bed sheets with you? They tend to get somewhat dirty, and can harbor fleas, mites and ticks, parasites that can all be transmitted to you or your children.

Do not allow your dog to jump up on you or others If when you came to my home for a visit I leapt up onto you repeatedly, you'd either leave or give me a poke in the nose. It would be an absurd, obnoxious way to greet you. Why then do so many dog owners tolerate the same behavior by their dogs?

Jumping up onto people is a leftover behavior from puppyhood, one never modified by the owner. Being small, excitable little fluff balls, puppies can't help but rise up on their hind legs to greet you, or to play raucously with other puppies or dogs. When small, dogs are actually encouraged by people to jump up onto their legs or laps. They get petted and praised for doing so. You've done it, right?

The problem is that the behavior never gets discouraged later in life, when the dog becomes too big for it to be a novelty. Then it becomes more than a bothersome intrusion; it becomes a means of challenging your leadership.

Coddlers inevitably have jumpers in the home, because jumping up is a symptom of poor leadership and humanization. Natural owners, however, instinctively know the behavior to be disrespectful, and as such understand that it must be discouraged.

To be a natural owner, you need to prevent your dog from jumping up on you and other persons. Here are a few ways of doing just that:

If your dog jumps up on you As with most behavior modification techniques, you have to elicit the behavior first in order to correct it. To do so, eagerly walk up to your jumping bean and give him a happy greeting, just enough to invoke the jumping behavior. When he does jump up, grab onto his front paws and hold them firmly enough to prevent him from pulling free, but lightly enough so as not to hurt. After about five seconds he will try to pull away; don't let him. Keep holding on while quietly talking to him about the weather or taxes or health care—as if nothing was wrong. In about fifteen seconds he will begin to frantically pull his paws away, and may even mouth you in the process. After a good twenty seconds, let go, while simultaneously saying "*Off!*" in a firm voice. Once he is on all fours, praise him and say "Good *Off!* " Then repeat the whole exercise. I guarantee you that after two or three sessions he'll never jump up on you again.

NOTE

If your dog has shown any overt aggression toward you, contact a professional dog trainer for help.

If your dog jumps up on others Sometimes a dog will only jump up on those who aren't around that often, to prove his dominance over them. To prevent this, you can have your friends practice the previously mentioned exercise, or you can take charge yourself. To do so, clip a leash onto your dog's collar, then have a friend come through the front door with a treat in hand. Lead your dog up to the person and, before he can jump up, have them ask your dog to sit in a firm but friendly voice. If your dog sits, have your friend give them the treat. If he jumps up, correct the dog with a quick pop on the leash and a firm "*No, Off!*," then walk the dog away. Repeat the entire exercise as many times as is necessary to achieve the desired behavior. The goal here is to teach your dog to sit when greeting strangers, instead of jumping all over them. Civil, yes?

Alternate methods to dissuade jumping If the other methods don't work for you, try one of these. Clip a leash onto your dog and leave it on him. Now, as in the first method, walk up and try to goad him into jumping up. At the same moment, casually step on the end of the leash, so that if he does jump, he ends up correcting himself. Just be sure to get the timing right, and to step on the leash at a point in which he will not have enough slack to actually jump on you.

A final method involves the use of a plant sprayer bottle filled with water. With sprayer in hand, goad him into jumping, then spray him square in the kisser with a tight stream of water, while simultaneously saying "*No, Off!*" Do this a dozen times each day and he will stop the jumping very quickly.

Never allow your dog to mouth you Another behavior learned in puppyhood, mouthing is a way for puppies to vie for dominance with their littermates, and to learn how hard they can bite before causing pain. It should not be encouraged no matter what age the person or dog.

When a puppy comes home for the first time, it will no doubt try to mouth its owners. Though natural, this should not be tolerated, as it leads to confusion for the dog regarding dominance. If you allow a dog to regularly mouth you, in his eyes it means you consider yourself a subordinate. Natural owners put a stop to this quickly; coddlers do not. You should assert your dominance by teaching your puppy or adult dog not to mouth anyone.

The moment your puppy or adult dog begins to mouth your hand, let out a god-awful yelp, as if bitten. Really project, with a high-pitched howl. It will shock your dog and make him aware that he has caused you pain. This is how pups in a litter learn to gauge their biting strength; it will quickly become an excellent way to limit the behavior.

If that method fails to work, try this: Whenever your dog mouths anyone, say "*No, no bite,*" then immediately place him into a crate in an isolated, darkened part of the home, and leave him there for fifteen minutes. Ignore any barking, howling or whining. Return to him only when he quiets down. Then bring him out again. Pet him on the head; if he mouths you, repeat the crate isolation. If he doesn't mouth, praise and reward him. Also, be sure to offer him your opened hand, encouraging him to lick instead of bite. By being consistent with this, he will soon understand that mouthing brings seclusion, while proper interaction brings praise and reward.

A final method you can use to dissuade mouthing is the good old spray bottle. Whenever he mouths you, give him a spritz in the kisser and say "*No Bite.*" Then pet him to see if he learned his lesson.

Some trainers recommend the "dominance rollover," or a hard shake of the scruff when a dog mouths improperly. I don't, as the typical owner usually doesn't know how to properly administer this type of discipline, and can sometimes get bitten severely in the process. I do sometimes use the technique on puppies I know will respond to it, but never on an adult dog, or on an animal that has shown any penchant for aggression. For you, it's best to use the techniques I've described. If they don't dissuade the mouthing, consult a professional.

Don't allow your dog to lean on, step on or mount you Some dominant breeds like to lean into or step on their owners in an attempt to establish dominance. Rottweilers are famous for it, as are Mastiffs and some other large breeds. Though endearing, it must be understood for what it really is, namely an attempt to use body posture to gain status. Dogs lean into, step on or mount each other regularly regardless of gender, to establish dominance, and will do the same to you if you let them.

Don't let your dog get away with it. Do what a dominant dog would; calmly push them off of you while saying "*No, Off.*" Don't be afraid to use your body as a dominance tool; just be sure not to hit or harm your dog while doing so. If he steps on your foot with his, remove yours from beneath his and place it atop his own! If he bullies you in any way with his body, exercise your dominance by turning or leaning into him, while taking an upright, dominant posture. Don't be a jerk about it; just let him know where you stand right from the beginning.

Many trainers, in an attempt to cater to the "coddling crowd," teach that this type of owner posturing is unfair and cruel. That's rubbish, in my opinion. No one is being harmed, and you are simply turning canine instinct back onto your dog. This is the truest nature of what I mean by becoming a proxy dog. If they teach each other with posture, what better way to teach them than with their own innately respected technique?

Again, the only caveat here would be with a clearly aggressive pet. Push a potentially dangerous dog off of you and you could get bitten, so in a case like this, avoid this posturing procedure altogether and get a pro to step in.

Avoid playing games that encourage dominance Too many dogs are taught to think they have pack parity with their owners due to seemingly innocent games played on a regular basis. As mentioned earlier, chase games which allow the dog to be the pursued should never be played. Instead, encourage the dog to chase you, and walk away if he tries to tease you into going after him. Tug-of-war should also be avoided, as it teaches a dog that he can vie physically with you, and sometimes win. Few activities erode an owner's leadership status more than this one. Children, especially, should be prevented from playing tug-of-war, as they are already low on the totem pole, and need all the status they can muster. Wrestling has the same effect so, unless you have clearly established yourself as the leader, avoid this as well.

Instead, find alternative activities that, while being fun, also reinforce your position as leader. Fetch, trick training, agility activities, or "find the cookie" sessions can accomplish this, as can an exercise I call the "boomerang recall," in which two or more people go to a secure area, spread out a bit and have the dog come to each of them sequentially. The dog comes to one person, gets a reward and praise, then is immediately called by the next person, and so on. It's fun for all, and helps reinforce the leadership of the human pack members.

The exception to this general rule comes when an owner has a particularly shy, submissive dog that actually needs to be raised up a tick in the confidence department. For these dogs, a bit of tug-of-war or chasing can actually help build self-assurance provided regular socialization with dogs and people is also included in the plan for the dog's "recovery."

Embrace a Canine Attitude and Awareness

Effective Canine Empathy

Dogs don't appreciate the heaped strokes of a Van Gogh, can't understand the inner workings of a jet engine, can't justify the rationale behind vegetarianism. Dogs cannot listen to a discourse on why child labor is unethical, then intelligently comment upon it. They can't because the limits of their cerebral cortex won't let them.

But we can smell the same smells, watch the same scenes and feel the same passions and loyalties they can. We can, if we try, understand why that terrier chased the squirrel up a spruce. We see a dog's tense body posture and know he is worried or contentious. We watch a dog stare out the window at the mail carrier and know that a bark is moments away. We sense a dog is forlorn over the loss of a family member. We can do these things. We can empathize with our dogs' perspective.

People and dogs feel love, loyalty, libido, courage, cowardice, fear, humor, hunger, and competition. It is in these affective, elemental commonalities that we can find the key to what I call *effective canine empathy*, or the ability to see things from a dog's-eye view. When we do so, our relationships with our dogs become clearer and wholly more rewarding than those based upon the false belief that our pets are silly little savants in fur coats.

The natural dog owner has the ability to adopt, at will, a canine "persona." That's not to say that, in an attempt to empathize with my dogs, I regularly get down on all fours and howl at the moon (although I have done so more than once). What it does mean is that I often try to see the world from their perspective. For instance, when I go to a dog park, I don't see the spectacle as just a happy, mirthful potpourri of playful dogs and their proud owners. I sense what my dog senses: the limping old Malamute who might not want a nose stuck in his butt; the frenetic Jack Russell terrier stealing a chunky Labrador's tennis ball; the slack-eared pit bull bitch with a near-healed horseshoe scar on her leg that still smells faintly of blood; the vibrant Shepherd mix with the scent of cookie crumbs still on her jowls. These are things that excite, motivate and direct a dog. These are things you should perceive.

Most owners fail at this. The worrisome body posture of an approaching stray dog, for instance, should alert you to a potential threat. But how many of you, when faced with a strange dog, choose to crouch down, look directly into his eyes, then reach your hand out to the dog's nose in a misguided attempt to convince the animal you mean well?

You might as well stick your hand into a meat grinder. Too many people think the appeasing "hand in the face" response is the right one; in reality, it is the surest way to get bitten that I know.

The right response depends on the situation. You should not worry about the angst of a stray dog, but instead be worried about your own safety. That's what your dog would do. If the stray just wants to be left alone, accede to that. Otherwise, calmly ignore him and let *him* decide if you are harmless or not. Look in another direction, as if you had more important things to think about. Let the stray sniff you if he wants. Then, if he appears to relax a bit, reach your hand into your pocket for a phantom treat then raise your hand up as if giving the "Sit" command. Say "*Sit,*" and see what happens. Such a display of confidence and expectation on your part will usually defuse the dog's fear enough for you to be accepted.

But what if, despite your actions, the dog's hackles go up and his tail goes stiff? What if he growls and advances? At that point, you should casually remove yourself from the situation while readying yourself for defense if need be. That means confidently crossing the street. If you have your dog with you, it means handing your leash off to a friend or family member if available and letting them walk off with your dog, while you do the same, albeit more slowly, in a flanking direction, to make the aggressive stray realize he now has two potential groups to deal with. It means being willing to kick the dog if need be, or swing a rock, chair, belt, keys, branch, purse, garbage can or hat at it—whatever is necessary to protect yourself and your pack members. It means reacting the way an alpha wolf would when defending his pack. Fights, though rare, are always possible, and must be planned for and dealt with.

If owners had the ability to read dogs the way other dogs can, situations like this would rarely become an issue. They avoid conflict by first discerning intent. That's the key; if you can learn to empathize with the canine condition, you'll make tremendous strides toward improving and enriching your relationship with your own dog. The purpose of Secret Three is to help you do just that.

Living in the Canine Moment

There is an immediacy to a dog's world, a real-time connection with his environment that humans can only envy. A dog goes outside and soon knows what the neighbors are cooking, which dogs are in their yards, what weather looms, which kids are walking by the house, and if the mail carrier has dropped anything off. He hears a juvenile crow tormenting his mother for food, smells fresh raccoon droppings atop the neighbor's garage roof, feels the sun warming the grass beneath his feet. The world as it happens moment-to-moment is accessible to him on a sensory level far beyond our own.

Few dogs spend time ignoring this sensory bounty in favor of daydreams and heady thoughts of coiffed collies bounding through a dewy meadow. Don't misunderstand; your dog does think ahead, plan, wonder, wish, long for, recall or miss. But he does so with regard to fundamental things; to you, to a lost companion, his coming dinner, the evening walk, the squirrel flitting about in the tree overhead. He does not wonder about the afterlife; he does not set long-term goals or envision what the house would look like painted blue. He interprets life with the intellectual and emotional capacity of a precocious three-year-old child.

From the time they are weeks-old pups rolling around the whelping box, dogs scrutinize their immediate environments with great expertise. They become intimately aware of status, safety, pack stability, territory and hunger, and, when old enough, sexuality. They acknowledge danger and avarice, and show prejudicial devotion to leader and pack. Roused by a moment-to-moment awareness, a dog's behavior is defined by these factors.

Dogs maintain a common-sense, tribal mindset to their environment, and to those around them. They sense a change, and quickly decide whether that change is beneficial or threatening to them. If the scent of a coyote wafts down into your dog's yard from a hilly wooded park nearby, he'll be instantly alarmed, and may bark, pace or whine. If he sees you rolling out the barbeque, he'll know from experience that yummy meats will soon fill the air with dog perfume, and will become animated and hopeful for a share in the bounty. When you sit down to put on your shoes, he'll guess that you are preparing to leave the home, and will get worked up over a possible walk.

If you are a sharp, observant owner, you'll notice these behaviors and often interpret them correctly. That's the purview of a natural owner, who can interpret things from a dog's-eye view. Natural owners live in this "canine moment" whenever around dogs; from a combination of experience and intuition, they have the ability to empathize and, if necessary, act.

How to Enter the Canine Moment

To learn how to enter the canine moment, one must first let go of the notion that your dog can interpret his world in abstract human terms. He can't; instead, he uses superior sensory abilities, body posture and concrete reasoning skills geared to the canine perspective. He could care less if you carp about him chewing up your slippers, or if the sweater you bought him doesn't fit well. He cares about things that affect him directly, in real time. When you accept that his world revolves around status, social interaction, safety, pack stability, territory and hunger, you'll be one step closer to being a natural.

Sharpen your senses You need to improve your sensory abilities, or at least pay more attention to them. Too many of us ignore or misinterpret common sights, smells and experiences; rest assured your dog does not. My goodness—there are dogs who can smell out cancer, bombs, or cadavers beneath the water! You'll never come close, but you can at least be more aware of how sensory inputs will affect your dog's behavior.

Take a few minutes to step outside. Smell the air, deeply. What do you sense? Flowers? Diesel smoke? Pork chops on a grill? The garbage truck down the street? You'll be surprised at what the meager human nose can sense when put to the test.

I have practiced exercising my olfactory senses for years, and can often detect and identify faint odors that others cannot. It takes practice, but it can be done. Being able to do so can often help explain canine behavior, or even predict it.

One bitter cold winter years back, a large male coyote came out of a nearby park to rummage through our suburban locale in search of food. On that same snowy day my stepson inadvertently left a door open, allowing my Rottweiler mix Louie to take a stroll around the neighborhood. After looking for him for hours, we returned home to find him sitting in the driveway, barking. As I approached him in the dark, I could clearly see he'd had a traumatic experience; he was all Rottweiler at that moment, ready for battle. Upon seeing me, he let go his dread and welcomed me home with a grateful sigh.

I immediately sensed a rank odor about him; he had in fact expressed (emptied) his anal glands, two glandular sacs just inside your pet's anus. The material secreted from these glands is foul-smelling, to say the least. Dogs sometimes secrete the contents of these glands when frightened or attacked; as Louie was a terribly confident, capable dog, I knew something profound must have occurred.

Something indeed had; I learned later the next day that the coyote had been seen in front of our house, and that Louie, in an attempt to defend his territory, had successfully defended his home and honor against the wily interloper.

I'd known as I approached Louie that he'd had an intense experience, simply from his smell and demeanor. Someone else might have concluded that he'd been rolling in excrement or tangling with a skunk; I knew better, based upon identifying the odor, and upon what it would take for a dog with such confidence to emit it.

Try to make the connection between what your dog smells, hears, sees, feels and tastes, and what he does. There is almost always a direct connection between sensory input and behavior; if you pay close attention, you'll begin to notice patterns, and will soon be able to predict his conduct. Be more aware of your own senses, too, especially when with your dog.

Watch and understand canine body posture Dogs communicate with each other through body posture. A natural owner knows this, and can determine a dog's intentions just from his physical bearing.

A happy, confident dog has a proud balanced stance with his tail up and wagging. He has a "smiley" face, with his mouth open slightly, ears pricked, and good eye contact. Contrast that with a worried dog, which will evidence a more crouched, stiff posture, with his tail tucked and ears down. He will tend to avert his glance, and may whine or bark. A natural owner will see the difference in a second, and respond accordingly.

A playful dog will bow down his front end to a companion, inviting the other to a fun romp. His ears and tail will be up and he may smile and bark happily. It's hard to miss the inviting posture of a canine clown.

Dominance posture is similar to the happy bearing, with the addition of some overt pushiness. A dominant dog may rest his chin atop another dog's back, or even mount, bump or swat at the other. Dominant dogs are easy to spot, as they are often initiating and controlling the actions of others.

Submissive dogs are worriers, and as such display the worrying postures mentioned above. They do so in order to appear smaller and less threatening to more dominant animals. They may even roll over onto their backs and urinate, or raise a paw up in a surrendering fashion. They may get chased away by more dominant dogs, or chase after more popular pets. They often display the whites of their eyes, and in general appear more stressed than more dominant animals.

When a dog is truly afraid, his hackles rise and his lips retract to show fangs. He arches his back a bit and tucks his tail, and may growl or snarl defensively. This dog is scared and wants to be left alone.

A truly aggressive dog may or may not raise his hackles, but not necessarily tuck the tail. He will snarl, sneer or bark, and will usually advance on his intended victim. This posturing suggests a dominant dog in the process of protecting territory, or a dog bred to display a high prey drive toward other dogs or persons. If you see this, odds are someone is going to get hurt. Best to take shelter in a home or auto, or at the very least find some defensive weapon to fend the dog off. Never run from a dog like this, as flight will only amplify his aggression.

A natural owner clearly understands his or her dog's posturing as it is happening. From there, it is simply a matter of taking the proper action to fit the situation. If your dog assumes a playful, confident posture, pull out the tennis ball. If he shows fear, determine what he's afraid of and remove it, then decide whether the fear was justified or not. If he fears a parakeet, there's something amiss, but if he shakes at the presence of a cougar, celebrate his good sense. If he shows dominant, pushy posturing toward you or your family, pull out the leash and do some training.

To really learn about how dogs posture, spend an hour at the local dog park without your dog. Just sit and watch the dogs interact. You'll be amazed at how predictable things can be if you just know what to look for. Once you become adept at spotting patterns, you'll more easily be able to know what your own dog is telling you with his body.

Discriminate between your dog's wants and needs What a dog wants and what he gets are often two different things. Drop a chocolate bar on the floor and your dog will probably try to eat it. But, as chocolate is extremely toxic to dogs, you would never want him to follow through with that desire.

A natural dog owner instinctively knows what his or her dog is capable of doing at any given moment. No matter how well trained my dogs are, I know they will try to eat that chocolate bar if given the chance. It's canine instinct. So when something like this occurs I instantly enter my "canine mode" and deal with the situation. I can't teach them that chocolate is toxic, but I *can* teach them that if I drop something on the floor, it is still mine, and that taking it from me would be disrespectful. To prevent this I teach my dogs the "Leave It" command, which simply tells them to leave be anything I deem off-limits.

I often hear clients make statements like *"my dog doesn't like it if I…"*. This is the quintessential coddler at work, one who hasn't yet developed effective canine empathy. From this statement alone I know this owner gives his or her dog whatever he wants, whenever he wants it.

What it also illuminates is the idea that a dog can direct an owner's actions, and perhaps even discipline that owner in some fashion to steer outcomes. Just how does a dog tell you that he *"doesn't like it?"* Does he growl, cry, bark, bite? Does he run away or urinate in the home? If allowed to determine what he does and doesn't like or want, a dog can quickly take control. That's why it is essential for you to know what he truly needs, and supply him with it and only it.

As a natural owner, be aware of your dog's true needs as well as his propensity for wanting what is harmful or inappropriate. He must have food at the proper time, must have shelter, must be kept safe from harm. And he must get leadership, respect and affection from you. But he need not have unlimited privilege, unearned praise or treats, or more food than he needs to live a healthy life. He needn't chew apart your belt or jump up on guests. He doesn't need to chase the neighbor's cat or sleep in your bed. He needs to be affirmed as a dog in your pack, not a toddler in your armchair.

To practice effective canine empathy, you'll need to understand what your dog wants, and determine if it is something he needs. If it won't adversely affect his health, upset the established pecking order in your home, or harm or disrespect another, it should be allowable. But, if any of these things will be influenced, deny him the opportunity. That's what the alpha wolf would do.

Embracing Loyalty

Though a simple concept, canine loyalty isn't always understood, especially by dog owners who pamper or spoil. Coddlers treat their dogs as humans, and as such can inadvertently reject the canine social construct in favor of a more progressive, humanistic model, one that shuns prejudicial loyalties; desirable for humans, no doubt, but detrimental to dogs.

Loyalty to one's pack is as elemental to a dog as breathing; without a prejudicial allegiance to one's group, social cohesion would no longer be possible. All manner of behavioral problems would occur, leading to chaos.

You belong to a pack. Though consisting of animals and humans, it is a pack nonetheless, especially in your dog's eyes. This pack is the core of your dog's competence; it is his raison d'être.

In order for you to understand the world from a dog's perspective, you must embrace this idea and do whatever you can to support and nurture your pack. If you are to truly "be the dog," you must revere the pack mindset and show prejudicial loyalty to it, even if it means sometimes going against common sense.

Let me explain. Imagine that, while at the park, your dog steals a stranger's sandwich and runs off with it. Obviously the sandwich is not his, and must be replaced by you forthwith. But disciplining your dog for the rude theft is *your* responsibility, and not the stranger's, even though he was wronged. If you allow the stranger to discipline your dog, you would be showing disloyalty to your pack.

The "doggish" thing to do would be for *you* to instantly discipline your dog, letting your dog know that the leader of his pack is upset with his dangerous, improper behavior. If instead, the stranger were allowed to discipline him, it would show your dog that you are a paper tiger, and not capable of disciplining or defending your pack. It would create doubt and worry in your pet's mind, and weaken your authority.

How to Embrace Loyalty

To truly embrace a canine attitude, be loyal to your pack and to the ideal of leadership. Above all, make all discipline your responsibility, or the responsibility of another human pack member.

If a strange person or dog tries to hurt your pet, defend yourself and your dog to the best of your ability instead of expecting him to go it alone. Just your attempt at defense will create a sense of unity between you, unique to the pack mentality.

Be steadfast in your desire to keep your dog safe and secure, both in and out of your home. A loyal leader "dog-proofs" the home; this means no toxic plants or chemicals; no dangerous, exposed wires; no potentially unsafe foods; no open doors, windows or gates; and no threatening or diseased animals.

Loyalty also means being there for your dog when he needs you; when sick, injured or frightened. It means spending the night driving through the neighborhood looking for him if he gets lost, or finding a 24-hour veterinary emergency clinic at three in the morning. if he is in need of medical attention. It means taking your responsibilities as the leader literally.

Loyalty means being dedicated and reliable, just like an alpha wolf who would spend the night looking for a lost pup, bring food to a sick or injured pack member, defend the pack from invasion, find food when it is scarce, and see that the pack's home territory is free from hazards.

Poise and Sincerity

Dogs respond to character and honesty better than do humans. It's one of the reasons we love them so much, and why natural owners fair better than coddlers. Natural owners exude a sense of integrity; their interactions with dogs are straightforward, truthful and frank, just as those of an alpha wolf. Amongst dogs and their natural owners, "PC" is an indecipherable waste of time.

There is something about a natural owner's bearing and deportment that dogs sense immediately, a confident, pragmatic style that attracts respect, obedience and relaxed behavior. It's part of the reason why the dogs of natural owners seem so much calmer and more thoughtful than those of coddlers.

Poise and sincerity are key qualities respected by all dogs. Owners who project these invariably have fewer behavioral problems than those who allow their emotions to dictate how they interact with their pets. A poised, sincere owner reserves undue emotion for only the most dire of circumstances; opting for patience, understatement and consistent example to get points across. Even when disciplining a dog, the natural owner rarely loses his or her temper, or shows unnecessary emotion.

A natural owner shows sincere gratitude whenever his or her dog behaves well. For instance, when your dog sits quickly upon hearing the command, you should sincerely praise him. Be genuinely impressed! Your praise will be taken as thanks and acceptance, two attributes that go far in the dog world. So, when your dog comes when called, plays fairly with other dogs, or stands by patiently while you groom him, show your sincere appreciation by praising and rewarding, and by telling him calmly just how appreciative you are.

Never break a promise to a dog. For instance, if you are in the habit of rewarding him with a walk after dinner every evening, try your best to do so, as he expects and looks forward to it. The consistency of a natural owner is a promise of sorts, an unspoken contract that dogs rely upon. They adore consistency and routine; become erratic or unpredictable and your dog will lose confidence in you.

The natural owner's consistency with rules is another important indicator of poise and sincerity. If you punish your dog one day for barking yet praise him the next for the same behavior, you'll lose his respect and confuse him. Applying different rules to two dogs in the same home is also a no-no; what goes for one must apply to both, in order for you to appear fair and competent.

Think about how much more pleasant it is to work for a calm, thoughtful employer, rather than one who constantly flies off the handle for the slightest reason. One creates a relaxed, respectful work atmosphere, while the other guarantees high turnover and gastric ulcers. Be that composed authority figure and you'll see a major change in your dog's attitude toward you.

Why Calm Indifference Gets Results

Many clients of mine have owned dogs that go ballistic whenever someone leaves or enters the home. Though a certain amount of excitement on the dog's part is natural when someone comes or goes, a full-out behavioral meltdown is uncalled for, and often symptomatic of owner error. Incessant jumping, barking, spinning or dashing about is obnoxious and unnatural. When taken to the extreme, these manic dogs can even evidence excited urination, destructive behavior, or even redirected aggression.

This type of abnormal behavior is often caused by the owner's insistence on encouraging a manic, overblown greeting or departure ritual whenever he or she leaves or returns. The departure often goes something like this:

"Okay, Cuddles, I'm going now, but don't worry, I'll be back soon! Be a good boy! Oh I love you sooo much!! I'll miss you! Watch the house for me! Take care!"

The greeting ritual is often just as saccharin:

"Oh Cuddles, did you miss me? I missed you sooo much! Give me a kiss! Oh yes, yes, yes! I'm sorry I was gone so long! Want a cookie?"

This affective owner behavior teaches the dog that departures and greetings are hectic, disturbing events, and that acting out is the desired reaction to them. The dogs are inadvertently taught to become overexcited whenever someone leaves or enters. This leads to exaggerated, overblown, obnoxious behavior, like a child throwing a tantrum whenever its mother leaves the room. It's classic separation anxiety, dog style.

Though tempered somewhat by the dog's personality, the main cause of this behavior is a coddling owner who injects too much emotion into the greeting/departure ritual. He or she feels bad about leaving or overexcited about returning, and as such inflates the passion of the moment. The owner focuses a selfish tirade of attention onto the dog, causing the heightened, frenzied reaction.

Overreacting or paying too much gratis attention to your dog contradicts the attitude a competent leader should project. In a wolf pack, the alpha pays only the amount of attention necessary to discipline, protect, nurture or teach his subordinates. It is in fact the more submissive members of the pack that pay constant attention to the more dominant wolves, a way of paying homage to their elders and supporting the status quo. The alpha that fawns all over lower members of his pack won't stay an alpha for very long.

Effective owners develop an attitude of "calm indifference" toward their dog. It's a bearing of enlightened reserve, a stoic presence that in practice actually causes dogs to perk up and pay attention. Like a worldly supermodel that knows all eyes are upon her, the true leader uses a measured diffidence to control, and influence.

A dog or person in a position of authority who appears to pay scant attention holds a very powerful card. It's an alluring pose, and a sign of primacy recognized by all canines. To truly understand effective canine empathy, you'll need to embrace this "hard-to-get" bearing.

In truth, natural owners who exude this nonchalant attitude are actually very attentive and loving to their dogs' needs. It's more of a performance, really, an act designed to calm, defuse, and focus. A natural owner knows that less is more, that staying calm and somewhat reserved will serve not to alienate, but rather to regulate and temper the dog's attitudes and actions. It creates a certain aura of mystery about the leader that insures obedience and calm deportment.

The right way to handle greetings and departures is to defuse them, or reduce them to simple, unemotional actions. Before I leave my home, I hide a few treats about the place for my dogs to search out while I'm gone. In time, this transfers the focus away from me leaving, to them finding treats. Once ready to go, I simply say "*see you later*" and leave, without drama. When I come home, I don't even greet them until I'm in the home and settled. Then I'll have them sit, give them a quick pet, and go about my business.

For dogs that have learned to go ballistic, I tell my clients to use the treat-hiding exercise, and to then *completely* ignore them when leaving or entering the home. Only when the dogs finally settle down should they get any attention at all. If that takes two hours, so be it. The idea is to never reinforce crazy behavior with attention of any kind.

To be a natural dog owner, you should embrace the alpha wolf's habit of displaying calm indifference, especially during greetings or departures. Your dog will learn to pay better attention, and begin to see you in a more respectable light.

In Praise of Predictability

Earlier I spoke of how important routine and ritual are to a dog's peace of mind. Indeed, the unpredictability or sudden absence of key desirable events in a dog's life can cause stress, leading to misbehaviors of all kinds. If, for instance, a dog's owner petted him one day for licking him, then punched him the next for the same behavior, the dog would soon become neurotic. Likewise, if a dog used to being fed at six found the schedule changed to nine, then four, then not at all, stress would result. I sometimes vary feeding schedules with my dogs as a form of thought-provoking enrichment, but not on a regular basis, and never on a dog with behavioral abnormalities.

Pack life is dependable. Like a child who knows a parent will be there to pick her up from day care, knowing when something pleasant or necessary will occur can be a real comfort to a dog.

Just as regularity creates confidence and security, unpredictability can build anxiety, a major source of misbehavior in dogs. For example, a client of mine with a shy, high-strung Dalmatian abruptly switched from working at home to commuting to a nine-to-five job every day. This required her dog to move from being in the home most of the day to living in the fenced yard for upwards of ten hours at a time. Already susceptible to stress-related misbehaviors, the Dalmatian began barking and whining incessantly, digging cavernous holes in the lawn, and chewing obsessively on the chain-link fence until a tooth cracked. The sudden move from home to yard, in combination with the apparent abandonment of her by her owner, generated the anxiety-spawned meltdown.

The solution entailed the help of technology, and the cooperation of a neighbor. First, the dog was brought back into the familiar confines of the home. Second, I had the owner record a soothing twenty-second monologue into a tape recorder that held a one-minute endless loop tape, the kind used in older answering machines. I had her place the recorder in her bedroom; just before leaving for the day, she'd turn the recorder on playback, so the dog could hear the soothing sound of her voice through the closed bedroom door, playing and replaying itself every forty seconds at low volume. We then got a neighbor to come over twice a day, to let the dog out and socialize a bit.

These techniques worked well in calming the dog down, and in easing her owner's angst. Over time we had the owner lower the playback volume ever so slightly, until after a month or so it was no longer audible, or necessary. Then we installed a magnetically-locking doggie door on the back entry, one which opens only for a dog wearing the proper electronic triggering collar. After a few weeks of training, the dog learned to use the door to go outside when necessary, then come back in to the security of the home. The neighbor still came over, albeit once per day instead of twice, insuring good housetraining and sociability.

How to Maintain a Predictable Environment for Your Dog
Predictability isn't hard to maintain for the intuitive natural owner.
Following are some suggestions:

- Once a feeding schedule is determined, stick to it as closely as possible. Also, try not to change the type of food served too abruptly, as this can cause housetraining issues. If a change of food is required, do so gradually over a two-week period. Only after a dog is behaviorally sound and reliably housetrained should you consider altering the feeding schedule.

- Walk your dog around the same times each day. Feel free to vary the route, and also perhaps the persons or dogs encountered.

- Try to leave and return home around the same time each day to create a secure, predictable mindset in your dog, and to also prevent housetraining accidents. If you are delayed, have someone familiar to your dog fill in.

- If you have regular play sessions with your dog, try to keep them up. Your dog looks forward to them more than you know.

- Maintain a fair, consistent style of interaction with your pet. Punishing him one day for something then letting the same behavior slide the next will only serve to stress him out and damage your authority. Similarly, letting him get away with misbehavior a few times (like jumping up), then randomly punishing him for the same behavior later is unfair and inconsistent. Avoid gross variations in temper or volume; instead, stay cool, avoiding emotional outbursts whenever possible.

- Try to avoid surprising your dog with unexpected stimuli, such as the sudden appearance of another dog or cat. Instead, ease your dog into new relationships by introducing him to the new characters for brief periods of time, on neutral territory away from home.

There are exceptions to this general rule. Once your dog has shown himself to be well adjusted and confident, you can vary surroundings and scheduling somewhat, in an attempt to enrich his environment and stimulate his mind. For instance, the sudden appearance of a veterinarian-approved chew toy, or the random placement of treats about the home, though unpredictable, can prove a great addition to your dog's day. Or, walking him to a new park or down a new street every so often can also be productive. Before varying stimuli, though, be sure that your dog has first developed the confidence and security that comes from a consistent, predictable lifestyle.

A World Without Grudges

Dogs don't hold grudges. They forgive and forget better than any other species I know. It's one of their most admirable qualities, one we humans could learn from.

Accidentally step on the tail of a cat and he'll hate you for the next twelve years. Do it to a dog and he'll probably yelp, then look at you as if to ask "*What did I do wrong?*" Unless the dog has profound fear or dominance aggression issues, he'll quickly let it go and get back to the business of being a dog. They hold little resentment, and have the forgiveness capacity of the most pious.

Resentment amongst wolves would be counterproductive, considering how important their social dynamic is. They must cooperate in order to function as a pack. Grudges serve the isolationist cat much better, and as such are incorporated into the feline psyche. Generally solitary except for mating, they zealously guard hunting territories, and fare better when left to their own devices.

Humans are passionate about holding grudges. We become offended more easily, perhaps due to a wider range of potential grievances, both real and imagined. Politics, religion and a host of abstract social mechanisms often combine to create anger and bitterness that can last for generations. Somehow, though, we manage to stay together despite the bad blood.

To better identify with your dog's perspective, try not to hold grudges against him. For instance, if he chews up your slippers, discipline him properly, put away all leather items, then let it go. Don't stay mad for the rest of the day, because it just doesn't make sense to him. He won't know how to process your resentment. If he has a housetraining accident, clean it up, take steps to prevent it from happening again, then let it go. Never stay angry with him.

Dogs don't goof up for spite. If anyone tells you otherwise, tell him that spite is a sophisticated human concept, one that the canine cerebral cortex just cannot grasp. Spite among dogs is fiction, and as such does not warrant resentment on your part.

I knew an ornery old salvage yard owner who adopted a male German shepherd mix to look after his yard at night. Upon coming into work one morning he found the yard gate wide open, thousands in merchandise missing, and the dog fast asleep in the office. Fuming, he threw the dog out of the office and refused to feed him for two days. For the next month upon coming into work, he'd call the dog a coward and kick him out of the office. After a month of this treatment, the dog ran away and was never found.

The old cuss treated the shepherd as if he were a human security guard, with the ability to understand that he'd done wrong by falling asleep on the job. The moral here is that coddlers aren't the only ones who make the mistake of treating dogs like humans.

Don't make that mistake. When your dog goofs up, deal with it as soon as possible; discipline if necessary, change conditions and interactions so that the problem won't happen again, and then *let it go.*

If you discover misbehavior long after the fact, don't even waste your time disciplining; the dog will not grasp why, eight hours after the fact, he's being punished. The closer to the time of the infraction, the more effective the discipline will be; if you miss it by more than a few minutes, just let it go.

With regard to housetraining accidents, the same basic rule applies. If the mess is hours old, don't call the dog over and stick his nose in it. That's old school nonsense that will only lead to a general fear of elimination by the dog. What you should do is bring the dog over, then *scold the mess*, not the dog. Doing so teaches the dog that you do not like the presence of such a product in your home. I know it sounds odd, but it's all you can do if you've missed the actual event. Then clean the mess up, apply an odor neutralizer (available at all pet stores), and decide why your dog had the accident in the first place. You may have given a young dog too much in-home independence too quickly, or you may have fed your adult dog something that he couldn't stomach. Or, you may have simply kept him indoors too long. It's your job to work it out.

If you do catch him in the act, you should scold him with a stern *"No! Bad Dog!"* That way he can associate the act with your displeasure. Pick up the mess and place it outside, near where you want him to eliminate. Do not let him see you handling the mess though, as he may learn that if you "handle" it he can, too. Then get him out there as quickly as possible and encourage him to relieve himself in that general area. If he does, praise him. Then clean up the indoor mess and reason out the possible causes for it.

Dogs don't hold grudges, so neither should you. Be a natural and let go of your anger and resentment; your dog will see this as a truly doggish attitude, and appreciate you for it.

Accept That Your Dog Has Responsibilities and Free Choice

Now, I'm going to come perilously close to applying human traits to dogs. It's okay though, because in this case it makes doggish sense.

Though much of your dog's behavior depends on canine instinct, breed, what you teach him and how you treat him, he still maintains a certain degree of behavioral autonomy. This is true of submissive wolves which, although allegiant to the alpha, still act according to their own personal needs and wants. When those needs and wants conflict with the alpha's, he disciplines and teaches; otherwise, they are on their own to choose. The alpha depends on them to instinctively choose what is best for the group without his always having to step in and correct. To do so would take up far too much time and energy. In other words, he expects his pack members to have a sense of self-control.

The idea that dogs maintain a certain sense of behavioral autonomy apart from human design differs somewhat from the more common assertion that a dog's actions are completely determined by breed and instinct, and by what humans teach him to do. I do not think this. I maintain that some decisions your dog makes are based solely upon his ability to weigh personal desire against pack necessity. In effect, the domestic dog often makes reasoned decisions on the spot, born of his own sense of protocol.

Removing personal accountability from a dog only serves to teach him that any behavior can be displayed without thought or decision, because it is the owner's responsibility to set all parameters. Most of us have not taught our dogs that ripping up the carpeting up is wrong; does that mean we cannot hold him accountable if he does? If my well-trained dog did this and I caught him in the act, I would of course discipline, then train him not to repeat the infraction; but I would also have to examine the cause for his surrender of respect and self-control. I would not hold a grudge, but simply consider why his sense of fairness and common sense abandoned him at that moment. A shard of cookie beneath the carpet would be an understandable explanation for the behavior if the dog were untrained, new or overtly disobedient; but a well-trained, established dog with good leadership? Not in my book.

Unlike most owners and trainers, I believe well-behaved, well-led dogs do have an inherent sense of self control and fairness, one which helps them make reasonable decisions on their own, instead of having to wait for an owner to micro-manage every act. As highly social beings, why wouldn't well-adjusted dogs have this pragmatic cognitive ability? Natural owners believe they do, and as such expect respect, fairness and personal accountability to be a two-way street.

In order to truly respect your dog, you must accept that he has responsibilities in his relationship to you and others in the home. He should be loyal and obedient, and behave within the parameters you have set. He should have manners, and treat all persons in the home with respect and deference. He should accept strangers and strange dogs you have welcomed into your sphere, but at the same time be prudently protective of your home territory. And he has a responsibility to think first before acting. He should have a sense of accountability *and* consequence.

Understand that he will often decide on courses of action all on his own, due to a sense of free choice and personal desire. For instance, if a squirrel runs across his path in the yard, he will chase after it without much thought. That is free will, fueled by predatory instinct. But if (and only if) you have trained him well enough, he should abandon the chase upon your command. If he does not, consider that not only disobedient, but impolite as well. He *made a choice* to disregard your wishes and should be disciplined for it, despite the strength of his predatory drive. After all, the entire premise of domestication requires the management and redirection of instinctive canine drives; to deny this would be to reject the very idea of domestication. Instinct should not trump the abilities of a skilled owner, and the obligations of domestication.

Natural owners, while understanding well the canine drives, do not make excuses for their dogs' bad behaviors. They accept that dogs have a certain "civic" responsibility to moderate their behaviors. And they know that respect and admiration, if not mutual, mean nothing. See your dog as a family member with personal responsibility and free choice, and you'll take a huge step toward really empathizing with the canine condition. Your dog expects no less from you.

Turbocharge
Your Dog's IQ

Why Educate Your Dog?

Want to make your dog smarter? If you do, it may be time for you to start teaching him his canine ABC's.

Though less developed than its human counterpart, the dog brain is nonetheless a powerful machine capable of fantastic reasoning and adaptability. Due in large part to evolutionary processes, the canine brain was given a great boost when archetypal canids began organizing into packs. The complexity and subtlety of behaviors and interactions inherent to packs eventually caused the dog's brain to grow into a sophisticated and sensitive problem-solving engine.

The reasoning portion of the brain, called the cerebral cortex, contains neural connections that allow higher brain functions to occur. Over the last few decades it has become clear to researchers that what we call "learning" is in fact the actual growth of new neural connections within the cerebral cortex. These connections allow more potential pathways for electrical current, and for the discharge of neurotransmitters, chemicals that allow communication between synapses, or nerve endings. The more pathways created, the smarter the animal gets.

Researchers have long known that education increases neural connections. Thus, the intelligence of your dog can be substantially increased simply by teaching it new behaviors and vocabulary, and by allowing the dog to experience as much as possible.

What dog owner would resist the opportunity to increase his or her dog's brain power? Certainly not the natural owner, who knows how training and enrichment activities make dogs smarter and happier. Unfortunately coddlers, though certainly loving toward their pets, rarely teach their dogs enough. This results in pets with below-average "IQ" ratings (if such a thing can be accurately measured in dogs). Though breed certainly plays a significant role in intelligence quotients, the least intelligent breeds will show more aptitude and adaptability than will the smartest, if given a superior education.

The dog with little training and experience has a less developed sense of awareness, and as such, when presented with a challenging situation, will tend to act out rather than think through the episode. This can result in misbehaviors ranging from housetraining accidents or excess barking, to destructive behavior or even aggression. At the very least, an uneducated dog will be poorly mannered and unpredictable. The dog that robotically barks or jumps up on people isn't thinking; nor is the one that blindly runs out the front door out into the street, or the one that refuses to come when called.

Educating your dog encourages him to be more introspective and well mannered. It calms dogs down and gives them behavioral options, averting the mindless behavior so common to coddled, untrained dogs. The educated dog is a pleasure and a real companion, a trusted friend as opposed to an obnoxious, tantrum-throwing two-year-old. The learned dog also gets to be with people more often, allowing better socialization and more quality time.

Natural owners build their reputations as leaders by consistently providing their dogs with intellectual stimulation. The owner/dog relationship becomes symbiotic, and more mutually satisfying. As in the wolf pack, owner authority slowly morphs from an "officer/soldier" arrangement to one of "mentor/student."

Well-educated dogs are safer, more trustworthy, and much more enjoyable than their naïve counterparts. Be honest now, which would you rather be with?

Essential Learned Behaviors

All dogs must complete elementary school before moving on to more advanced programs of study. What basic behaviors should your dog learn? I list nine essentials every dog should be taught as early on as possible to set the stage for a good relationship, get those neurons growing, and make future training that much easier. They are:

1. **Housetraining**
2. **Sit!**
3. **Down!**
4. **Stay!**
5. **Come here!**
6. **Leave it!**
7. **Give!**
8. **Loose-leash walk**
9. **Wait!**

In Secret Two: Understand and Apply Leadership, the Sacred Canine Code, I included sections on how to teach your dog to walk on a loose leash, and how to teach your dog to wait at a door or curb, or on a rug. Refer back to them to teach your dog these two vital behaviors. The rest of the basics I will cover here.

1. Housetraining

Your dog must be reliably housetrained in order for the pet/owner relationship to work. Unlike cats, which even as kittens have a near innate ability to eliminate in a litter box, dogs must learn to control their elimination habits. The first basic learned behavior, housetraining, must be taught to your dog by you.

Natural dog owners know when their dogs need to eliminate; they can see it in their behaviors. A puppy or adult dog that needs to go will become animated and sniffy, and will start instinctively searching for an appropriate place to relieve itself. This often occurs when the dog first wakes up, right after feeding time, and just before bedtime. The observant owner who develops a predictable, consistent daily schedule for his or her dog typically suffers few problems with housetraining issues.

Not so the coddler, whose dog can often suffer housetraining problems well into adulthood, making life miserable for everyone. The puppy or adult dog in question may choose to defecate or urinate in an inappropriate spot, possibly ruining carpets, bedding, or flooring. The undesirable spot they choose to eliminate in is often a closet, bed, or laundry pile, which provides the errant animal with materials in which to hide the "mistake."

Understand that a new puppy probably has no concept of what being housebroken means, as his mother or breeder cleaned up after him. It's up to you to teach him what your human expectations are.

Many owners attempt to paper-train their puppies; this method works poorly and only encourages elimination inside the home. Other owners don't even use paper, and simply try to keep an errant eye on the puppy in hopes of noticing just when he will need to go out. This method usually fails miserably. Some simply scream, yell, and strike their puppies when they have accidents. This is the best way to insure a puppy will never be properly housebroken.

A newly adopted adolescent or adult dog can also exhibit house-soiling problems. Perhaps used to being an outdoor pet, this dog comes into your home knowing nothing about your elimination protocol. Generally, an adopted dog has to be treated as if he were a puppy, with no housetraining skills whatsoever.

Often an unneutered dominant dog will exhibit classic *marking* behavior in and around his territory. Like wolves in the wild, he is staking out his domain to let all know of his dominance. This is common in coddling homes, especially with toy breeds, the most pampered of dogs.

A sick dog might temporarily lose control of his bladder or bowels. Often the urge to eliminate comes on too quickly for the sick pet to get to the proper area in time, causing an accident in the home.

The geriatric dog may gradually lose his ability to control urination and defecation. Sometimes the dog in question will urinate or defecate in his sleep. Though often treatable by your veterinarian, this problem often gets worse, not better.

The solution to your problem depends on your unique situation. Let's take them one step at a time.

New puppy or adopted dog with questionable housetraining Forget about paper training. Instead, take advantage of your dog's instinct to keep his sleeping area (or den) as clean as possible. To do so, purchase a plastic travel crate, available at any good pet store. When you are not able to directly supervise the puppy (or new adult dog), he *must* be in his crate. While in it, he will instinctively hold off on urinating or defecating. The new puppy or adult dog should also sleep in the crate, and be in it whenever you cannot be at home.

A puppy or dog can spend hours in a crate with no ill effects. Indeed, I will have a puppy sleep in one all night long with no problems at all. Coddlers, in an attempt to humanize, think of crate restriction as being cruel and avoid using them, to their disadvantage. Dogs of all ages actually appreciate the coziness of a crate; all my dogs always have one throughout life and can go in or out at will, treating them as sanctuaries. Just don't keep your dog in a crate all day *and* night, as this would be cruel.

The crate should be only large enough for your dog to stand up and turn around in. If it is too large, your dog will eliminate in the back and scrunch up in the front. This may mean purchasing one crate for puppyhood, and a second for when the dog grows into his full size.

Avoid an all-wire crate. Many dogs feel insecure and vulnerable in them. Instead, choose a plastic or fiberglass, airline-approved crate with a wire door and small windows but opaque walls, floor and roof. This gives a more secure feeling, and allows the dog to rest if others nearby are busy.

When home, keep the new dog near you if uncrated. *He should never be able to independently disappear into unoccupied portions of the home.* This is the primary cause of poor housetraining. This is the key!

To properly supervise, clip a leash on the dog and tie the other end to your belt loop; the puppy or adult dog will have to follow you around the home. You'll be able to watch him, and at the same time bond with him. When you suspect he needs to go, quickly take him outside.

Feed the new puppy or dog at exact times, to insure elimination on a reliable schedule. Free-feeding, or leaving food out all day can sabotage housetraining because it insures that food will always be in your dog's digestive tract.

Take the puppy or new adult dog out to eliminate first thing in the morning. Then feed him and take him out *again*. Puppies often have to go right after eating, so get into this habit to insure success. Also, always take your dog out after every meal, after play, and before going to sleep.

Take a young puppy out every hour on the hour during the day, to build the routine and prevent any accidents. Then gradually lengthen the time between potty breaks.

Just as your puppy or dog is about to eliminate, softly say "*Go potty,*" or "*Get in there,*" or whatever words you choose. You can even use different words for urination and defecation. If you do so, you will eventually get your dog to go on command, just by saying the words.

When your dog has an accident in the home If the accident has happened in the past few minutes but you did not witness it, clip the dog's leash on, bring the dog over to the accident, then *firmly scold the mess, not the dog*. Sounds nutty? Maybe. The idea is to let the dog know that feces or urine are *unwanted in the home*. If you scold the dog in front of the mess, he might think that the act of eliminating is bad, causing him to become stressed or secretive whenever the need arises. Scold the mess, then bring the dog out to a proper location and allow him to eliminate there, if necessary.

If you catch your dog in the act of eliminating in the home, clap your hands sharply and say "*No! Bad dog!*" then take him out (even if the event is still in progress) to the appropriate place to finish. Here you are correcting an ongoing misbehavior, so it's okay to scold. Just don't overdo it, and *never* hit.

If you take your puppy or dog out but he doesn't eliminate, bring him back inside and put him in the crate, or tie his leash to your belt loop. Wait fifteen minutes, then take him out again. Eventually he will go.

After following these instructions for a month, you should be able to slowly allow your new puppy or dog to have more freedom in the home. Let him be in a room away from you for short periods, gradually increasing that time as the dog matures. If at any time he has an accident, however, go back to the crate and/or the leash-on-the-belt-loop technique, and start again. Once the dog can go a full eight weeks without an accident, you have succeeded in housebreaking your pooch.

If the dog has an accident, make sure to clean the mess up thoroughly using an odor neutralizing cleaner, available at all pet stores. If you don't, your dog will home in on the scent and use the area for eliminating again. Remember, do not allow your dog to actually *see you cleaning up the mess,* as he might assume that it's okay to play with feces.

The marking dog The marking dog eliminates in the home because he wants to express his perceived dominance. Don't let him get away with it! To prevent marking in the home, try the following:

- **Have your dog neutered by the time it is a year of age to minimize domineering, territorial instincts. If your dog is not neutered, he will mark in the home, even if he respects you as leader. Even unneutered females will mark occasionally; having her neutered will minimize the chances of it happening again.**

- **Attend an obedience class with the offending dog. A dominant dog that marks in your home has no respect for you or the rules. You can change that by learning how to control him, and how to restore yourself as the leader of your pack.**

- **Correct the dog if he marks in your presence. Keep a short leash clipped to the offending dog's collar while in the home. If he marks, correct him with a firm pop on the leash and say "No!" Put him into a crate for an hour, then take him directly to an appropriate spot to urinate.**

• If you have been gone for hours and discover a wet spot, do not call and punish him, as this will, in fact, teach him not to come to you when called. Instead, bring him to the spot, scold the spot, then take the dog out to urinate. You will have to begin basic housetraining 101 again, as if he were a puppy. When you are gone he is in a crate or outside, period. When you are home he is tied to your belt loop or a doorknob, or in the room with you, leash on. After eight weeks without marking, he graduates. In the meantime, he sleeps in a crate and not in your bed!

The sick dog Never punish a sick dog for having an accident. Take him to the veterinarian for the appropriate treatment, then keep him in a crate when you are away until he is feeling better. If he eliminates in the crate, do not punish him. Simply clean out the crate.

The old dog An old dog will gradually lose housetraining skills. He is aware of the problem but cannot help it, and as such becomes worrisome and embarrassed. If you suspect age is the culprit, take your dog to the veterinarian; medications exist that can moderate incontinence. If medication can't help, you may need to create an outdoor dog pen with a concrete or pea gravel floor for him. If you experience cold winters, however, this may be hard on the dog, unless you can somehow heat the enclosure.

2. Sit!

Perhaps the most basic of behaviors, the act of sitting anchors the dog in one spot, helping to build attention. It's like teaching a child to sit attentively at a desk for the first time.

Choose a tranquil place at a time just before dinner, so your dog will be hungry. Then, holding a piece of cheese in your fingertips, place it near his nose. Slowly move your hand up and back, keeping it close to his nose, while at the same time saying *"Fluffy, Sit!"* His back end should naturally drop, and he'll be sitting. Immediately say "Good *Sit!*" Then hand over the cheese.

Repeat this often throughout the day. Eventually, you'll use either the rising hand motion or the spoken "Sit" command to get him to sit. After the dog masters the behavior, diminish treats until using them intermittently. Always praise for a good sit!

3. Down!

Also an anchoring, calming behavior, "Down" teaches a dog to tolerate being in a submissive posture. This helps solidify your leadership status and trains your dog to surrender control to you.

Start with your dog sitting and you crouched in front. Hold a piece of cheese in front of his nose; then, while saying *"Fluffy, Down!"* lower your hand down and away from the dog's nose. He should follow the cheese down. Feel free to apply gentle pressure on his shoulders if need be. Most dogs will at this point lie down; if he does, say *"Good Down!"* and give him the cheese. Then praise him!

With some dogs, you will need to vary the movement of the cheese. Practice it until you succeed. And always start treat training right before dinner! Soon you'll have your dog performing "Down" without treats. Just say *"Fluffy, Down!"* as you drop your hand in front of him. As with "Sit," you'll soon be able to use either the hand signal or the verbal command.

4. Stay!

Teaching your dog to stay in one spot is a revolutionary concept for many owners. Imagine controlling the actions of an energetic dog for thirty minutes! Natural owners know the importance of this behavior, one which more than any other establishes authority over the dog.

The "Stay" instruction helps the dog learn that he need not stick his nose into every little thing that happens around him. It teaches him to observe passively and *think* about what's going on, instead of neurotically involving himself. When a dog develops the ability to calmly watch behavior without participating in it, you'll know that his brain is learning to focus and analyze. That's learning, my friend!

Sit-Stay! While living in Los Angeles years ago, I spent afternoons training my prodigal dog Louie, then just a pup. One of our weekly sessions took place near a busy trucking company loading dock, on a narrow ribbon of grass that lay between incoming and outgoing semis. I'd work on Louie's sit-stays there, to hone his performance in the face of great distraction. Bystanders would do double takes upon seeing the big Rottweiler/Shepherd mix doing a perfect soldier-sit while Peterbilts and Kenworths streamed by on both sides. The truckers soon came to expect him there, and would toot their air horns in tribute.

Begin to teach "Stay" with your dog in the sitting position, leash on. Once he is sitting, tell him *"Fluffy, Stay!"* while simultaneously holding your open palm in front of his face. At first, stand a few feet away while holding the leash up loosely. After just three or four seconds, say *"Good Stay!"* then call him to you, praising and rewarding with a small treat. To help keep his focus, wave a small treat around in the air; move it up, down, in and out—just enough to keep him anchored. Handlers at dog shows use this technique during examinations by the judge; it helps immensely. Work this a few times, attempting to get him to keep the sit for a brief period. If he breaks the sit position too quickly, say *"No!"* with a slight upward pop on the leash, then start again.

Gradually lengthen the time your dog stays in the sitting position, and your distance from him. Softly say *"Good Stay"* while he keeps the position. Walk around him while he is sitting, still holding the leash in case he breaks. Eventually you'll be able to drop the leash and walk around the room.

Try not to keep him in a "Sit-Stay" position for more than a few minutes as, unlike the "Down-Stay," it can become uncomfortable. Also, always release him from the "Stay" with a quick touch on the head; this lets him know to never end the "Stay" on his own without you first touching him. It makes for a more reliable "Stay."

Down-Stay! Once you have your dog performing a reliable "Sit-Stay," apply the same principle to the "Down" position. Dogs can maintain a "Down-Stay" for long periods; I often have mine fall asleep doing them. The longer duration will allow you to truly teach your dog to relax, focus and trust.

With his leash on, have your dog lie down. Then simply tell him to "*Stay,*" using the same open-palmed hand signal you did with the "Sit-Stay." If you have mastered the "Sit-Stay," he should be able to hold the "Down-Stay" position for at least a few minutes right away. Hold onto the leash at first, albeit without tension. If he breaks position, correct him with a slight pop on the leash and a simultaneous "*No!*" then put him back into position again. While he holds the "Down-Stay," praise him by saying "*Good Stay.*"

Gradually lengthen the time he stays in the "Down" position, and your distance from him. After a week you should be able to drop the leash, walk around him, and even leave the room for a few seconds without him breaking.

Once he gets good at staying in a "Sit" or "Down" position, begin introducing mild distractions to test his focus and obedience. Have a person walk by. Drop a treat on the floor ten feet away. Have someone knock on the front door (a hard one). If he breaks, correct and replace him in the exact same position. Eventually, move the behavior outdoors to perfect it. Use a leash at first to prevent him from bolting.

5. Come Here!

Possibly the hardest behavior to reliably teach a dog, the recall or "Come Here" is also one of the most important, as it insures that your dog will return to you if he gets off the leash. The hardest part of teaching the behavior is that, at some point, you must teach it off leash. That means you'll have no recourse if the dog decides to ignore you and take a hike. He would in effect be reinforcing his own bad behavior and learning that you, a slow human, cannot do anything about it.

To prevent this, you first need to insure your role as leader. Dogs who respect their owners and recognize them as leaders will return to them because they *want* to, not because they have to. The natural's dog understands this; the coddler's does not.

Here's how to teach the "Come Here." By the way, I call it "Come Here" instead of "Come," because adding the *"Here"* lightens up the sound of your voice a bit and makes the dog more likely to respond. Too many owners bellow out the word *"Come!"* in such a way as to scare the dog; adding the lilting *"Here"* gives the command a happier sound.

With your dog on a leash, get six feet away then crouch down and enthusiastically say *"Fluffy, Come Here!"* Make yourself as inviting as possible. If your dog does not respond, correct and say *"No,"* then happily say *"Come Here"* again. If he comes, say *"Good Come Here"* then reward with a treat. Work this in different areas for a week until your dog reliably comes. Be sure to start praising the dog for coming to you *the moment* he begins to approach.

Begin to include minor distractions, like a person or other pet in the room. Work until the dog reliably comes to you every time, still on leash. Correct if he ignores you. There can be *no option* but to come to you, as the leash is on. If you have to reel the dog in, do so. Be positive when the dog comes!

Now use two leashes clipped together, a ten- or fifteen-foot piece of rope, or an extendable leash. Repeat the same exercise only from farther away. Continue until he always comes to you. Correct if necessary.

Find a twenty-foot lead and continue until he responds every time. Try it at a park, with few people and no off-leash dogs present.

Find an enclosed area, like a vacant fenced tennis court. Work the "Come Here" on a long lead a few times. Then take the lead off and try it from ten or twenty feet away. If successful, praise and reward. After two or three successful attempts, go home. Remember to stop the training while your dog is *still eager to perform*. If your dog does not return to you, walk him down (do not chase), clip the lead back on, correct and say *"No,"* then repeat the *"Come Here"* on leash. After success, again try it off leash. Do not move on until he comes to you every time.

Finally, try it in a fenced yard or park. Do it on leash a few times, then try one or two off-leash attempts. At first, have no distractions present. Work it randomly, and increase distractions over a two-month period. Always praise! Reduce treats after the behavior becomes consistent. And *never* call your dog to you then punish him, as this will teach him not to come!

6. Leave It!

At some point you will need to prevent your dog from touching something, either because it doesn't belong to him, or because it might be harmful. A sock or child's toy, for instance, or a dropped chocolate bar.

Coddlers often have problems with their dogs being overly possessive of objects. The dog may grab some dirty laundry, play keep-away with it, and then growl or snap when someone tries to take the object back. This is typical behavior for a humanized dog, taught that he has parity in the home. Possession equals high status, in the dog's mind.

As the natural leader, you have dominion over *all* objects in the home, including your dog's toys, chews, treats and food. You should be able to handle anything without him objecting, provided you are not unfair about it. Once you develop true canine empathy, you'll understand this instinctively.

Teaching "Leave It" to your dog isn't hard. First, place a toy, a sock, and a treat down on the floor in a large, quiet room. Now clip your leash onto your dog's collar and walk him briskly around the room on a loose leash. Let him get within a few feet of each distraction; when he begins to go for one (but before he actually gets to it) say *"Fluffy, Leave It"* in a commanding voice, while continuing to walk briskly. If he ignores you and goes for the object, correct him with a moderate pop on the leash and a verbal *"No!"* Then say *"Leave It"* again. Keep moving and working the command until he begins to consciously avoid the objects; when you see him make an effort to avoid an object, praise him by saying *"Good Leave It!"* Then give him a treat.

Continue the on-leash training for a few weeks, setting him up with various tempting items in differing areas. Then place a treat on the floor and let him into the room, off leash; when he heads for the treat say "*Fluffy, Leave It*," and see what happens. If he leaves it alone, praise him, pick up the treat, ask him to "*Sit*," then give it to him. If he ignores you and eats the treat, say "*No, Bad dog!*" then clip the leash back on and work the behavior again. After a week, try it off leash again. Eventually he'll get the idea. Remember; you must have dominion over items in your home!

7. Give!

If your dog gets hold of something he shouldn't have, you must be able to take it from him without drama or conflict. The "Give" command gives you that power. It conditions your dog to know that *you* decide what is and isn't okay for him to have.

Many coddled dogs show possessive aggression when an owner attempts to take back a sock, remote control, candy bar, or any number of objects a dog shouldn't have. Spoiled into dominance, these dogs believe they have the right to possess anything; as "leaders," they think it's their privilege to control.

Natural owners know better. They can take anything from their dogs without fear of aggression, because the dogs trust them, respect them, and subordinate themselves naturally. And, they understand that a natural owner won't be unfair or prejudicial. They know a darn good reason must exist for the owner to want that thing back.

To teach your dog to give something back, consider first teaching him to fetch a ball or stick and bring it back to you. In doing so you'll be playing a fun game that he likes, one that involves letting you have the ball back, so you will throw it again and again. He will naturally learn to release the ball to you in order to continue the game.

It's quite easy; just find an object he likes, then, starting indoors, throw it a yard or two away and say "*Fetch!*" When he goes for it, immediately begin praising, saying "*Good Fetch!*" Then get down low and call him over, while holding a treat in one hand. When he comes over, casually grab hold of the fetch object with one hand, while offering the treat with the other. As he lets go the object, say "*Give*," then "Good *Give!*" Increase the distance the object is thrown until, after a week, he is retrieving it from across the room. Then, move it into the yard. Once he gets it, reduce treats but keep praising. He'll soon learn that surrendering the object insures fun, and the chance at a treat.

In the home, prevent the need for wresting an object away from your dog by keeping the home dog-proofed. Pick up all clothing, baby toys, and anything else the dog should not have access to.

If your dog gets hold of something forbidden, never chase after him, as this will only become a game he likes. Instead, call him over, have him sit, then casually take the object in your hand and say "*Fluffy, Give.*" If he doesn't, resist pulling, as it could either turn into a tug-of-war, or else incite a growl. Instead, blow a quick burst of air into his nose then immediately say "*Give.*" Most dogs will let go of the object at this point; when he does, praise him verbally but don't reward with a treat, as you don't want to make it into a game. Save that for teaching the "Fetch" command, the best way to guarantee your dog will give something back on command.

Outdoor Behavior Essentials

In ways, the outdoor learning arena is the more influential location on canine IQ growth; it's unpredictable and dynamic, and therefore more challenging to your dog's mind. Spontaneous social situations, off-leash opportunities, variations in weather, and a potpourri of sensory stimuli all serve as a grand laboratory for your little pal. And what happens to your dog outdoors usually happens to you as well, allowing you to show-case your potential skills as a natural dog owner. So, being outdoors serves not only as a learning experience for your dog, but for you as well.

Walks No other activity helps bond owner to pet as much as a simple walk around the block. It's your own miniature wolf pack on patrol, exploring your extended territory, dealing with whatever comes your way. The amount of sensory stimuli, experience and confidence-building that occurs can't be duplicated in the home or yard; for your dog, it's the "real world," and a great simulation of what wolves do every day.

Your dog's IQ can receive a big boost from simply taking him out twice a day on a ten- to fifteen-minute walk about the neighborhood. It allows your dog to experience new sights, sounds and smells, and to meet people and pets he otherwise might never get the chance to meet. Compared to "shut-in" pets, dogs walked every day are more likely to be happier, calmer, and smarter than dogs who aren't walked regularly.

A walk with your dog should be as safe as it is entertaining. So before you begin, scope out the planned route. Choose a ten- or fifteen-minute course in your immediate neighborhood, free from hectic activity. For instance, don't choose a route passing a yard with ferocious Rottweilers or pit bulls, or an area with chaotic traffic or construction activity.

Select a route that takes you by quiet homes, with some foot traffic about. An elementary school with kids playing fifty yards off is fine, as is passing by a park with parents and toddlers milling about. Make a note about where the yarded dogs are located, and whether or not they are friendly or highly territorial. Barking dogs are a normal part of neighborhood life and should be included in your dog's education; vicious fence biters should be avoided, though, especially if your dog is insecure or has a tendency to overreact to displays of aggression.

Require your dog to walk beside you on a loose leash during the walk. Remember, it's your walk too. Don't use an extendable leash, as they encourage pulling and teach your dog to ignore you. Use a six-foot leash, which requires your dog to pay attention to you.

Don't let your dog decide when and where he will relieve himself. Make that *your* decision. If you let him decide, it sends a message that you are just a passive servant instead of the natural leader. And, letting your dog eliminate in an inappropriate place can be rude to neighbors and pedestrians; better to decide for yourself, and then dispose of the waste in an appropriate manner. To do so, you'll need to have a plastic bag available, so always take one along, tied to your leash.

Before crossing a street, make your dog wait at the curb for a moment, either in a sitting or standing position. If practiced for a few weeks, your dog will develop the habit of slowing and stopping at every street corner, a habit that might one day save his life.

After you develop a nice walking routine with your dog, consider throwing in a bit of variety. Turn down a different street or change the route slightly to include more foot traffic. Take a few treats along, and have friendly passersby offer one to your dog in exchange for a nice "Sit." This will build his trust in others, and teach him that accepting other humans is not only okay, it also can be profitable.

By gradually varying the stimuli during your walks, you'll desensitize your pet to unpredictable events, raise his confidence levels and build his experience. All that equates to a smarter, more seasoned dog.

During the walk, randomly work your dog's obedience. Have him sit, lie down, stay—whatever he knows. Doing so away from the familiar confines of the home will generalize the behaviors, making them more solid and reliable.

Every so often, take your dog for a walk of an hour. The extra stimulation and exercise will benefit both of you. Take other family members along, or friends with well-mannered dogs of their own. Insist that your dog walk calmly beside you during this "extended family" walk; no dog-on-dog playtime until you reach an appropriate venue.

During walks, insist that your dog remain well mannered and thoughtful toward you and others. No jumping up on passersby, no barking, no pulling on leash to get to another dog—nothing disrespectful to your position as natural leader.

If during your walks you encounter dogs with questionable temperaments, *do not* feel obliged to greet them. Some owners feel guilt over consciously avoiding other owners and their dogs, even if it is to avoid a potentially aggressive incident. Don't be so politically correct; as a natural leader with canine empathy, your intuition about other dogs is laudable and necessary. If you doubt the safety of an approaching dog, simply cross the street, wave to the other owner, and walk on. Do so confidently, without fear. Remember, it's okay to profile in the dog world!

In the car A good number of dogs never properly learn how to ride in a car; often they are simply tossed in with no conditioning or desensitization, resulting in all manner of undesirable behavior. Barking, territorial aggression, anxiety, destructive behavior, and even car sickness can occur, ruining the experience and teaching the dog to hate the car.

See things from the dog's perspective; a dog inside a moving vehicle feels insecure because the very "ground" he stands upon is unstable (this happens in elevators too). Unpredictable starts and stops cause him to constantly adjust his stance to maintain balance and control. A dog can develop motion sickness from this, a negative experience he associates with the car. Once that happens, the dog begins to hate riding anywhere.

The other issue is what I call the "fishbowl effect." A car is basically a windowed container, much like an aquarium; a dog inside one can feel somewhat exposed to outside events. He can see what's happening but cannot interact, much like a dog in a fenced yard. This can cause anxiety, barking, destructive behavior, and territorial aggression. If you've ever walked by a car with a snarling dog in it, you know what I mean.

Natural owners know that because the car is an exposed, unnatural environment for a dog, desensitization must first occur before the pet can relax and enjoy the ride. Here are some basic suggestions you can follow to make riding in the car an easy experience for your dog:

- **When getting a puppy or adult dog, teach him that the car is a great place to be. The best way to do this is to feed him in the parked car, with the engine off. Wait until a half hour after his regular dinnertime, then bring him out to the car. Open the back door or hatchback, place the food down, and encourage him to jump in and chow down. If he's too small to jump in, place him in. Praise him as he eats. At first, keep the door open, but hold onto his leash.**

- **For the next session, close the hatch or door and sit in the driver's seat. After he finishes eating, praise him, then go back inside the home.**

- **Continue, except now start the engine when he is about halfway done with his food. If he stops eating, just sit calmly; do not comfort him, as this would be interpreted as a** reward for being worried. Just sit there; he should get back to his meal. Repeat for at least two or three days before moving on.

- Next, begin taking him out to the car several times each day. Put him in, start the engine, and give him treats and praise. Do so at least twice per day, for a few days. At this point you can stop feeding him full meals in the car. Let each session last for at least five minutes, and consider having friends or family walk by the car randomly, to desensitize him to pedestrians outside.

- Next, put him in the car, toss some treats or a toy into the back, then put the car in gear and drive slowly up and down the driveway, or in the street in front of your home. Drive smoothly, with no sudden braking or turning. Do this twice per day for at least two days before moving on. From this point, schedule the sessions at a time when he has as little food in his belly as possible, to minimize the chances of vomiting.

- Increase the distance you travel. Remember to praise him, but consider eliminating treats at this point. Within three days you should be able to drive around the neighborhood without him getting ill or worried. After a week, take him for a longer drive, perhaps using the freeway. Visit a friend fifteen minutes from your home, or go visit your veterinarian. Once there, praise your dog for not getting ill or anxious.

- From this point, I recommended keeping your dog in a travel crate while in the car. In addition to protecting him and you in an accident, the crate will keep him still and prevent him from watching the sights go quickly by, a factor that increases the odds of him becoming ill or anxious.

- Drive to the parking lot of a supermarket and sit in the car with your dog for ten minutes as people walk by. Give him a treat or two, and plenty of praise. Then take him for a walk around the lot, letting people offer him treats for a "Sit."

If done in slow, deliberate steps, your dog should eventually learn to enjoy the car. Just make sure that he goes for at least two or three rides each week, to keep his "auto immunity" up.

The Power of Vocabulary

Guide dogs for the blind must have a minimum vocabulary of eighty-six words in order to properly perform their jobs. That's more than some people I know. Seriously, the smarter a dog is, the more words he understands. Dogs that work as service or show animals, compete in obedience trials, or serve the police or military all have extensive vocabularies, in accordance with their complex training and great responsibilities.

I once calculated how many words my old dog Louie knew, and came up with a preliminary list of over a hundred. Eventually I discovered even more words that he knew, words he had learned without me realizing. For instance, whenever I'd ask a family member if they'd seen my *keys*, he'd immediately come over to me, thinking it meant we'd be going out for a ride in the car, something he loved. *Keys* meant fun. The same applied to *shoes* or *food*.

The more words and associations you teach your dog, the smarter he'll get. Take the time to actually count the words he currently knows. Most dogs know at least twenty; a list of basic words most dogs know probably includes: *Good, No, Okay, Cookie, Come, Sit, Down, Stay, Off, Get, Walk, Outside, In, Water, Catch, Eat, Potty, Leave it, Sleep, Fetch*. That's twenty right there. And of course, all dogs know their names.

Try to triple that. To do so requires you to first get his brain engaged through basic obedience training. Teach him *how* to learn. Get him to want to participate and focus. To be a natural owner demands it.

Your dog learns new vocabulary through association. When he hears "Cookie" and is then given one, the association between the word and the pleasant gift soon becomes apparent. It's a positive event preceded by a key word; he quickly identifies the unique sound of "Cookie" as the lead-in to a treat.

Your dog learns vocabulary through negative associations as well. Though fewer in number than the positive words he knows, negatives such as "No," "Quiet," "Get" and "Leave it" serve to decrease undesirable behaviors that can sometimes occur, either through instinct or because of unplanned reinforcement. Your dog learns the meaning of "No," for instance, when you associate the word with some type of corrective action, like the removal of a desired item, a leash correction, a squirt from a plant sprayer bottle, or just a simple change in the tone of your voice from sweet to authoritative.

The difference between the use of a positive word like "Good" and a negative like "No" is that the negative is *always* followed by a positive word as soon as the dog ceases the bad behavior. This allows the dog to understand the behavioral options he has; he can choose his fate through deciding upon his own behavior, and the consequences that follow. In contrast, a positive word like "Cookie" is an end unto itself, and as such needs no follow-up vocabulary.

Teach your dog new words through repetition and reinforcement. For instance, teaching a dog to "Sit" requires you to use the command often while attempting to initiate the desired behavior, and then consistently rewarding with a treat or praise.

For a dog to learn a new word, you'll have to regularly teach him new behaviors, develop a consistent routine, and gradually expand his exposure to new things. For instance, he won't learn "Swim" unless you repeatedly take him to a body of water. He won't learn the agility word "Weave" unless you take him to agility classes and work on the behavior each day. He won't learn "Leave it" until you purposely set him up for possible failure or success by routinely placing prohibited items on the floor and training him to ignore them.

Teaching your dog new vocabulary will give him an expanded lexicon to draw from. Once he has this his IQ will swell, as will your appreciation for his intellectual abilities. Remember; a dog should not be just a reactive automaton; he should be a thinking individual with focus, curiosity, and the ability to understand consequences. Giving yours an extensive vocabulary will insure he will exercise these abilities.

Above and Beyond:
The Value of Advanced Training

Natural owners understand that the more diverse and challenging a dog's training, the smarter and more well mannered that dog will be. A dog with advanced training will better integrate into its environment than will a dog taught just the bare essentials.

To complete your dog's education, you'll need to take him past grade school and get him a college education. Doing so will broaden your relationship, and build admiration for your dog, taking natural ownership to a new level.

Let's look at some advanced training options you can teach your dog.

Basic Obedience with Distraction,
Varied Environment, and Group Behaviors

Once your dog can reliably perform basic obedience behaviors, take him to the next level by perfecting his performance in more challenging environments, with unpredictable conditions. For instance, a dog trained to perform a reliable "Down-Stay" in a quiet room probably won't be able to do so in a room filled with strangers. Even a change of venue to a friend's home can be a trial to a dog not used to new surroundings.

Equally demanding to a dog is the challenge of performing basic obedience behaviors while in the presence of other dogs. Adding this social variable to the mix can truly test a dog's abilities; for that reason, trainers always like to work dogs in the presence of pets of similar behavior levels.

Once your dog can perform a reliable "Sit-Stay," "Down-Stay" and loose-leash walk in and around your home environment, begin introducing distractions into the mix. Try it on leash at the local park, with people and dogs walking by. Tempt him by throwing toys or treats onto the floor in his vicinity, or by having an energetic ten-year-old skip through. Doing so creates a real-life scenario that will ultimately generalize the behaviors. That's why I worked my old dog Louie at the truck loading dock; if he could hold a "Sit-Stay" with Peterbilts roaring by, he'd hold it anywhere, anytime.

When you first begin to increase distractions, you'll find your dog breaking position often; that's okay, and normal. Remain patient and avoid undue emotion. At first just say *"No!"* when he breaks, then repeat the exercise, making sure to reward with a treat and praise when he finally gets it. If he continues to break position, add a light corrective pop on the leash when you say *"No!"*; otherwise stay calm. The key is to *increase distraction gradually*, so that he will have the best chance at succeeding.

Off-Leash Obedience

Working your dog's basic obedience with his leash off involves a high degree of learning and trust. Dogs that obey commands without the failsafe control of a leash are doing so because they want to please and impress their owners. No leash is needed to play "Fetch" with an eager Labrador retriever, because the breed lives to retrieve; the same principle can be applied to any well-trained dog that wants to perform.

A dog that performs flawlessly off leash can be trusted not to bolt off into the street if his leash does happen to come loose. In fact, off-leash competence builds focus and trust for both dog and owner; there is nothing quite as gratifying as when you *know* your pet will walk by your side down a crowded street without bolting or ignoring you, no matter what happens. You become wired into each other.

A feeling inherent to all natural owners is one of immense faith in the loyalty and competence of their dogs, once properly educated. I *know* my dog will not run away, or ignore me because of some enticing distraction. It is an immensely empowering feeling!

Coddlers rarely experience this. Their dogs inevitably take off as soon as the leash is detached; they are the pets with embarrassed owners always chasing after them at the park. These dogs are not trustworthy because they have not been convinced of anything but the belief in their own self-importance.

To be a true natural owner, you should teach your dog to behave and interact without the restraint or excuse of a leash.

First, begin working your dog's on-leash manners in public venues such as parks, promenades, and city streets. Instead of a relaxed loose-leash walk, however, you should begin teaching a more official "Heel" command. The difference lies in the focus level of your dog; with a loose-leash walk, all he need do is keep from pulling, and walk with his shoulders near to parallel with your legs. But with a "Heel," he must pay meticulous attention to your every move; if you stop, he must stop and quickly sit beside you. When he is on "Heel," his shoulders must be precisely in line with your legs. "Heel" is much like soldiers marching in lockstep; it requires great focus for the dog, and as such should not be worked for more than a few minutes. If you made your dog "Heel" for an entire thirty-minute walk, he'd be exhausted by the time you arrived home.

Heel To work "Heel," first be sure he will reliably walk on a loose leash in public. Then, take him to a quiet sidewalk and have him sit beside you, on your left side, both of you facing the same direction. With the leash held in your left hand (a bit closer to his collar than normal, still loose, but with slightly less slack), say *"Fluffy, Heel,"* while simultaneously giving the hand sign, a fast sweep of your right hand that begins above his head and moves forward, toward the direction of the "Heel." You can use any hand signal you want of course; this is simply a sign used by many.

Step forward with your left foot and begin walking with purpose and good speed. Your dog needs to learn how to begin walking with you, at this pace. After ten feet, stop abruptly and immediately say *"Fluffy, Sit."* Practice only this start and stop for the first day, making sure he sits with every halt. The "Sit" should become a near soldierly act, with his rear planting itself quickly. Once he grasps the added intensity of the exercise, you'll be able to slowly return full slack to the leash.

Some trainers use a treat dangled in front of the dog's nose to get the exact position and attention level; I do not. This "carrot/mule" approach shouldn't be needed if you have already taught a loose-leash walk. It also tends to create too much focus on the treat instead of the trainer. Simple praise and a treat at the end should suffice.

Once he perfects this quick, precise "walk-and-sit" maneuver, begin lengthening the walks and varying the speed. Realize the "Heel" is simply a loose-leash walk, with instant responses and a "Sit" at every pause.

Gradually add unpredictable about-face and right-angle turns into the mix. Turn left *and* right. Be patient, and understand that your goal should be to get your dog to grasp the heightened attention and focus required of the exercise.

Now, when you stop abruptly, instead of saying "*Sit,*" simply stop. If you have worked it properly, he should "Sit" without being told. If he does not, say "*No, Sit!*" then "*Good Sit*" once he does. The aim is to get him to sit automatically whenever you stop, without you asking.

Work the "Heel" twice each day for five minutes, under varied situations. Then take your dog to a fenced-in area (such as a vacant tennis court) and begin to work the "Heel." Make no turns; just walk at a medium pace for about twenty yards, back and forth. During one of these legs, casually lay the leash atop your dog's back and keep walking. If he's getting it, he will just keep walking in a tight "Heel" without missing a beat. After ten yards, stop, and see what happens. He should "Sit" nicely. If he does, praise him mightily and give him a treat. If not, go back to on-leash work for a day or two, then try again.

Soon you should be able to put your dog into a "Sit," unclip the leash, then begin working the "Heel." Start making wide turns to the right and left, then slowly tighten them up. Slap your thigh and say "Heel" if he begins to drift a bit out of position. If need be, reattach to the leash.

Finally, take your dog to a residential area with low traffic and work the off-leash "Heel." Do so only once he has shown himself to be reliable, and obedient regarding the "Come Here."

Linking off-leash behaviors Once you have perfected the off-leash "Heel," you can move on to other off-leash behaviors, eventually linking them together. For instance, after working "Heel" for a few minutes, clip your leash on him, put him into a "Down-Stay," drop the leash then walk a few yards off. Don't back away as if he were a bomb; just casually amble off, watching him with your peripheral vision. If he breaks position, calmly say *"No,"* then re-place him into the "Down-Stay" in the same spot. Keep working it until he'll do it reliably with no leash involvement at all.

Next, while working his off-leash "Heel," have him stop and "Sit," then tell him to "Wait," using the hand signal, a palm in his face. Casually walk off a few yards; watch him peripherally, but act indifferent. Then crouch down and happily call him to you. When he comes over, praise him and reward with a cookie. Work these random "Waits" everywhere, with increasing levels of distraction. Increase the distance you put between you and your dog, until you can stand fifty yards off without fear of him breaking or running off.

Never advance until a behavior is perfected. Push him just enough each time to encourage intellectual growth, like a muscle being worked out properly. If you have doubts about his recall abilities, err on the side of caution and return to earlier training in more secure surroundings.

Aim for reliable off-leash obedience within six months of the start of "Heel" training. Once you arrive at this level, you'll feel a natural connection to your dog never before experienced.

Changing Handlers

A dog's ability to learn is often limited by his inexperience with other handlers. A dog showing perfect obedience with his owner will frequently perform poorly or not at all for someone else, even if it's another adult in the family. This limits his intellectual growth and versatility.

Getting your dog to perform for another person is much like you or me learning a different language. Before we do so, we may vaguely feel the limitation, but don't truly understand its significance. When we finally do become fluent in another language, though, the increased ability to communicate with others becomes exhilarating.

Teaching your dog to perform for another person will do this for your dog. He will at first be confused by the person's different posture, attitude, voice and style, but that's okay; he will catch on. Once he does, his versatility will be accentuated as will his tolerance for others.

Choose a friend or someone in the family. It should be someone the dog trusts. Spend some time working your dog's basic obedience in front of him or her, to make sure the basic techniques you use are understood. Then go for a loose-leash walk, with the other person on your right and the dog on your left. Work his basic obedience a bit, then, while walking, casually hand the leash over to the other person and switch positions. Keep walking for a bit; then have the person begin working "Sit" and "Down" randomly, punctuated by walking and turning. If your dog has difficulty obeying at first, try giving the commands yourself while the other person simply holds the leash.

After this, have the person take your dog out on his or her own. All the basic on-leash behaviors should be worked in a casual, low-stress manner. The objective is to get the dog's brain to appreciate the different ways in which other persons communicate.

In addition to expanding your dog's communication skills, working with new people will also help generalize the concept that all humans are dominant, and not just you. This is a huge issue with coddled dogs who, though usually responsive to their owners, rarely take other people seriously. As a result, coddled dogs, while being kenneled or "babysat" for by friends, often exhibit disobedience, fear, separation anxiety or even aggression. Teaching your dog to like being worked by others will prevent this. Remember: a natural owner realizes that, for his or her dog to be truly safe and well adjusted, the dog must feel comfortable interacting with other capable persons.

Trick Training

Teaching your dog tricks is a great way to increase your dog's IQ. After just a few days of trick training, you'll notice his attention and focus increasing; he'll become more eager, willing and self-assured. Timid dogs will perk up, while bossy dogs will begin to pay attention. What could be better?

No corrections or negative reinforcements are needed or desired when teaching tricks. After all, tricks aren't necessary to your dog's safety, or to your position as leader. They are simply fun behaviors designed to boost your dog's learning power. In addition, they will expand your insights into dog training, fostering within you an inventive mindset.

Natural owners teach tricks to their dogs because they are a bonding tool and a way to get a dog thinking out of the box. I'm including two simple tricks here, ones you should be able to teach your eager student in no time. Give them a try! One piece of advice: teach tricks for short periods, and always stop while your dog is still raring to go.

Shake Put your dog into a sitting position in front of you, then crouch down in front of him. Have some treats handy. With your left hand, lift one of your dog's feet while saying *"Fluffy, Shake!"* As you shake the paw, say *"Good Shake,"* then reward with a treat. Practice this for a few days; eventually your dog will grasp that shaking gets rewarded.

Next, instead of grabbing his paw, tap on the back of his wrist joint while saying *"Shake"* to entice him into raising the foot on his own. Any movement of the dog's paw should be followed by reward and praise. Work this for a few days before moving on.

Gradually reduce the tapping pressure to the back of his wrist. The objective is to get the dog to lift its paw upon the anticipation of your offered hand. Soon he should lift his paw on his own. Reward any movement of the paw at this stage, and be positive!

Once the dog willingly raises his paw, begin to offer your hand from a foot away. This becomes the hand signal for "Shake." You want to get the dog to respond to the command without being touched. Reward any positive responses on his part. Eventually he'll offer up his paw upon your saying *"Shake."* Within two weeks, he'll get it.

Once he gets it, try using only the verbal command, or just the hand signal. You will eventually get him to respond to either.

After he perfects "Shake," reduce treats and increase verbal praise. Giving treats sporadically at this point will actually improve the dog's performance, because it encourages a *heightened expectation*, like gamblers playing a slot machine.

Speak "Speak" can be challenging to teach, because you can't really show your dog how to do it (other than by barking at him). Rather, you must wait for him to bark, or else find a trigger that provokes him to.

Find a circumstance that causes your dog to bark. The doorbell, a knock at the door, vigorous play—whatever gets him to vocalize. I've gotten dogs to bark by blowing into their nose, or by barking at them during play.

When he barks, simultaneously give a hand signal; I use a fist tapping at the air. The reason to use a hand signal *before* any spoken command is so the dog won't get confused listening to you and an inducement sound (like a doorbell) at the same time. Also, if you have to blow on him to trigger a bark, you can't speak at the same time.

If your dog barks, immediately reward with a treat and praise him. Any vocalization from him at this point is great.

Work this for a few days. The goal is to slowly remove the inducement action and get him to bark only with the hand signal. You'll *bridge* from one to the other. Once he barks on the hand signal, begin using the verbal command *"Speak"* in conjunction with the hand signal. Here you'll be bridging between the hand and verbal signals.

Work "Speak" until you can get him to bark with either the hand or spoken command. Then reduce treats, increase your distance, and work the trick in different locations. And remember: it's all for fun!

Enrich Your Dog's Environment

Your Dog's Fed Up and He Can't Take It Anymore

In the past, zoo animals in cramped cages had little to do but eat and pace. As a result, many developed a host of medical and behavioral problems, among them anorexia, obesity, neuroses, infertility, unpredictable aggression, antisocial behaviors and ineffective parenting skills. Denied their natural habitats and behaviors, wolves, lions, bears, elephants and apes could not interact with natural environmental stimuli, and often became listless and troubled.

Today, zoologists know better. They work hard to enrich the lives of captive zoo animals through innovative enrichment programs that re-create experiences in the wild, relieving the boredom captive creatures often suffer as a result of not living in their natural environments. Clever animal behaviorists design diverse habitats and activities that mimic conditions in the wild, resulting in a calmer and more dignified frame of mind for the animals.

These enrichment programs strive to reproduce the conditions *and the challenges* that captive creatures might experience in the wild. A leopard cannot be happy, for example, unless it hunts each day. Leopards denied this activity become dull, listless and unpredictable, and often refuse to mate or feed. They need to feel the excitement of the hunt in order to be mentally and physically healthy.

To that end, zookeepers no longer simply place food in the same spot at one certain time; instead, they move the food, hide it, or put it in a place that is difficult to get to, such as high up in a tree branch. In this way, the leopard has to call upon its innate physical and mental prowess to secure a meal. This stimulates its mind and gives it a sense of purpose, both essential to optimal health. The same goes for zoo polar bears, who fish for their dinners out of stocked trout pools, or for elephants, who play with suspended, honeycombed beer kegs filled with food pellets.

Domestic dogs need to feel the same type of purpose. Unfortunately, most live in environments similar to those of captive zoo animals from the forties and fifties. In comparison to wild canines, their territories are minute, and the behavioral stimuli offered to them nearly nonexistent. Their natural instincts to hunt, stalk, play or investigate are rarely engaged, and often discouraged.

Most dogs spend their time sleeping, wandering around an empty home, or pacing inside a fenced enclosure in the backyard, much like a stir-crazy zoo leopard or coyote. Starved of sensory input and intellectual stimulation, these dogs can develop a host of behavioral or physiological problems ranging from overeating or aggression to obsessive-compulsive disorders, separation anxiety, destructiveness, antisocial conduct, or out-right disobedience or aggression.

Even when home, owners often do not relieve their pet's boredom, as they themselves usually fall into predictable behavior patterns that exclude the pet's well-being. Unchallenged physically or mentally, dogs become dullards or problem pets.

If zoologists can invent enrichment programs that minimize the boredom and neuroses of captive zoo animals, so too can the owners of domestic dogs. By introducing simple objects and activities that challenge and stimulate the dog's mind and body, owners can give their pets a feeling of purpose, perhaps for the first time in their lives. These enrichments occupy the pet's time, teach him to focus and problem-solve, tap the pet's natural intelligence and curiosity, and serve as an outlet for pent-up energy, imagination and stress. A calmer, happier, more directed dog will not become bored, negative and listless, and will be healthier and better behaved.

The natural dog owner knows this instinctively. Able to empathize with his or her dog's yearning for purpose and exploration, the "natural" turns his or her home into a stimulating place, to appeal to the dog's curious, busy nature.

The coddler confuses enrichment with pampering. Rather than giving their dogs what *they* need to feel whole, coddlers give what is needed to make *themselves* feel happy. Trust me, dressing a Chihuahua up in a tutu and sending him to the doggy pedicurist is the last thing the pet wants. It's unnatural and insulting, and not at all enriching to an animal wanting to be treated like a dog and not an ingénue.

From Wolves to Shut-ins

In the wild, wolves lead a challenging, diverse lifestyle. They hunt, mate, play, raise young, maintain social order and defend the pack and territory from predators and other wolves. There is not a waking moment wasted. This complex lifestyle ensures that the wolves' minds and bodies remain stimulated virtually all the time, guaranteeing good physical and psychological health. Wolves rarely get bored, overweight, depressed or self-destructive, and are seldom needlessly aggressive toward other pack members. They remain alert and intelligent because *that is what their environment demands of them.*

Not so for the domestic canine. Most do not hunt, mate, raise young, or participate in complex social hierarchies. They have relatively minute territories, few distractions, and extremely limited routines. Though safe from the dangers of the wild, our dogs rarely get to sample nature's abundant and developmentally vital stimuli.

Many of us leave our dogs alone for up to ten hours each day, in homes or yards. They become bored hermits whose lives revolve around eating, sleeping, and waiting. Tolerable to a cat, this solitary lifestyle is extremely hard on dogs, which crave the same attention, diversion, and mental stimulation that we do.

Our society now provides captive zoo animals with plenty of environmental stimuli, to keep them happy and fulfilled. Shouldn't we treat our domestic dogs with the same level of care and respect?

Enrichments

You needn't be a zoologist to enrich your dog's environment. All that's needed is some imagination, a few toys and treats, and various items found either at home or in the pet store. If done consistently, your dog's species-specific behavior will be stimulated, making him happier and better adjusted to his environment.

The enrichments are broken down into two categories, *environmental* and *behavioral*. Environmental enrichments include any unique objects or individuals introduced into your dog's environment, or subtle changes made to the home territory. Each of your dog's five senses will be stimulated by these changes, as will his prey and territorial drives. Behavioral enrichments include any unique stimulating activities you involve your dog in, such as visits to the park, swimming, or even hide-and-seek games.

Environmental Enrichments

You can make your dog's home "territory" a more enriching place to live simply by introducing fun, stimulating items and changes for your dog to experience. For instance, whenever I leave a dog alone in the yard, pen or home, I will supply some fun distractions designed to stimulate one or more of his senses. Following are some suggestions for environmental enrichments you can use, categorized by your pet's senses.

Visual enrichments Compared to his olfactory and auditory abilities, your dog's vision isn't his most acute sense. Nevertheless, random visual changes to his territory can be a great way to stimulate his imagination and keep his brain engaged. I'm not including toys and chews here, because they fall under taste or prey-drive enrichments. Some good visual enrichments include the following:

> • Leave the television tuned to a station with dog or cat programming. Keep the sound just loud enough for your dog to hear the audio. You can even rent a pet-themed DVD or videotape and play it for him while you are gone!

- Install several safety mirrors around the home, mounted at "dog height," so your pet can check himself out. Most dogs think it's another pet, making for interesting encounters! Remove mirrors if he becomes destructive or aggressive.

- Hang a few large, moving mobiles about the home, at a height that he cannot reach. Attach one to a slow-moving ceiling fan if you have one. Color matters less than design; feel free to use photos of pets, or even yourself.

- Randomly rearrange the furniture in one room. Even a subtle shift of position can pique your dog's curiosity. The purchase of new furniture will also stimulate his interest.

- Purchase real or artificial plants and place them about the home. If he digs in the dirt or tries to eat them, relocate them up high. Also, be sure to avoid toxic houseplants such as aloe vera, poinsettia, fern, lily, dieffenbachia, philoden-dron and agave. (Note: This is a partial list only; please consult your veterinarian for a more complete listing.)

- Stock a ten-gallon aquarium with active fish and place it in sight but out of your dog's reach. Make sure it is lighted. He should find it amusing.

- Leave a curtain or two partially open, to allow your dog a view. If he is a barker, though, avoid this enrichment, as it may increase the unwanted behavior.

- Move paintings and prints to different locations on the walls, or purchase additional ones and hang them.

- Vary the lighting in the home while you are gone. Having certain lights go on and off automatically by means of a timer will get him thinking.

For dogs left in the yard or pen during the day, randomly adjust those environments as well. Move his doghouse or water bowl, or leave safe, random objects scattered about.

Olfactory enrichments Your dog's nose is the sharpest in the land; to take advantage of this, provide plenty of olfactory enrichments for your dog in and around the home. These can include the following:

- Leave trace amounts of lavender oil, cinnamon or allspice about the home or yard. Most zookeepers use this in their wolf enclosures, and the wolves seem to love it. Consider leaving a trail of one of these, leading to a rewarding dog cookie!

- Hide a few bouillon cubes about the home or yard; the aroma will get your dog searching. The same can be done with minute amounts of sprinkled instant soup mix. Avoid using too much of either though, as their sodium content can be somewhat high.

- Place a freshly-cut evergreen bough in a vase up high; its fresh, powerful aroma will make your dog think he's hiking in the woods!

- Place some coffee grounds inside a paper bag and leave it just out of your dog's reach. He'll be craving a cup of "joe" when you get home.

- Dab a hint of vanilla extract onto a few small bits of paper and hide them about the home. Like the lavender and spices, he'll seek them out.

- If your dog spends lots of time in the yard or pen, dab tiny bits of lard, bacon fat or canned dog food about. He'll search for the bounty for hours.

- Hide a few hairs from another dog (or a cat) in random places. Your dog will wonder where the interloper is; this healthy "stressor" will stimulate him mightily. You can do the same with feathers or even a friend's hair or sweat! If your dog begins to mark over these samples, though, discontinue them.

Auditory enrichments Dogs have a superior range of hearing to humans. While we can perceive sounds ranging from 20 to 20,000 Hz, a dog's hearing ranges from 40 to 60,000 Hz, or nearly triple ours. In addition, their larger, multi-directional ears can better "funnel" sound, helping canines locate prey.

You can stimulate your dog's auditory world in these ways:

- Leave a radio on in a closed room tuned to classical music or talk radio. Your dog will think that someone is home. You can also set your clock radio alarm to go off randomly while you are gone, tuned to talk radio or classical. Avoid harsh music, though, as this can upset some dogs.

- Purchase a thirty-second-long endless-loop audio tape (the type used in older answering machines). Record yourself saying something ("Hi, Fluffy, are you being a good girl?"); then, when you are ready to leave the home, place the tape into a tape player located in a closed room, push play, then leave. Your five- to ten-second message will play repeatedly while you are gone. You can record other sounds as well; try the voice of another friendly person, birds chirping, or even a wolf howling!

- Purchase a "sounds of nature" tape or CD and play it at low volume for your dog while you are away.

- Randomly call home while gone and leave a message for your dog. Be sure to turn up the volume on your answering machine so he can hear you. You can also use walkie-talkies to amuse him; set one in the living room then take the other outside with you and talk to your dog randomly from down the street!

- For outdoor dogs confined to a yard or pen, consider installing a small recirculating garden fountain somewhere out of the dog's reach. The pleasant gurgling will calm him.

- Also for outdoor dogs, try pointing a radio speaker out a nearby window and playing soft music or talk radio. You can also use the walkie-talkie technique.

Tactile enrichments Changes in how the home environment feels to your dog act as interesting stimuli, and keep him occupied. These can include the following:

- Randomly place small throw rugs of varying pile down about the house. Rotate their position every few days. These will stimulate him both visually and tactilely. Try adding olfactory enrichment by dabbing the rugs with lavender oil or sprinkling one with a bit of cinnamon.

- Vary the temperature of your home each day. The subtle changes will be noticed and evaluated by your dog.

- On warm days, leave a fan on low. The breeze will be noticed and appreciated by your dog. Just be sure to keep the fan and its power cord out of reach.

- Leave ice cubes in his water bowl. Their surprising texture and temperature will amuse him. You can even leave out a block of ice for your yarded or penned dog. Don't use dry ice though, as contact with it will injure your dog.

- Occasionally leave a kiddy pool filled with cool water out for your yarded dog. Tossing in a few ice cubes or a few buoyant, veterinarian-approved toys will give him something to play with.

- When you are home, randomly give your dog massages in exchange for a quick "Sit," "Down" or "Shake." The tactile experience will please him, and teach him to accept being handled.

Edible enrichments A common and effective enrichment, clever dispersal of edibles around the home territory can stimulate one of your dog's most elemental drives. Used by zookeepers to arouse prey drive and compel animals to find food, edible enrichments put dogs into problem-solving mode, something their wolf cousins do constantly.

Edible enrichments you can try on your dog include the following:

- Relocate your dog's food and water bowls, to make him search for his meal. Move them only a small distance at first, then gradually relocate them to different rooms or floors of the home. You can also elevate them, or place the food in three or four bowls instead of one. Let him search for it without help at first; only hint at the food's location if he fails to locate it after ten minutes. Use this enrichment only occasionally, to make the search worthwhile and challenging.

- Vary the amounts of food you feed your dog. One day give him two-thirds the normal amount, the next day give him a quarter more. You can even skip one day per month! Don't worry about this hurting him; unlike cats, canines can go for days without eating. When he gets his next meal he will "wolf" it down! Avoid feeding him excessive amounts though, as this might affect housetraining.

- Supplement your dog's diet with raw or partially cooked meats on a random schedule. Toss a chicken neck into his bowl, or give him a slice of fresh liver. Avoid bones, except for those in chicken or turkey necks. Never feed a dog cooked bones, as they splinter. Though a dog's digestive tract can easily handle raw food, consider microwaving raw meats for thirty seconds or blanching in boiling water for the same length of time, to kill surface bacteria.

- Randomly hide small treats about the house. Break a cookie up into five or six bits, then place them in corners, on stairs, under throw rugs, in his crate—wherever he's allowed to be. Once he gets into searching mode, reduce the number of treats and increase the level of difficulty in finding them. Ideally he should have to use his sense of smell more than vision to locate them. You can even leave a trail of crumbs that lead to a bigger treat, or to his relocated dinner bowl.

- Leave a few veterinarian-approved chews and chew toys about the home or yard. He'll savor them while you are gone. Avoid rawhide chews, as they can cause blockages in the intestines of some dogs. The compressed, "particle" type rawhide chews are okay, though, as are hooves, pig ears, and any nontoxic nylon-based chews. Regarding toys, use ones which your dog cannot destroy, unless you are there to supervise. Also, rotate toys from day to day, to keep your dog interested. Don't use too many at once, as he will become desensitized to them.

- Insert treats into a hollow, hard rubber chew ball and leave it on the floor. Your dog will go bonkers trying to get the edible prizes out of the toy. Also try smearing a small amount of peanut butter or canned food inside the same ball. Just make sure the toy is made of a durable substance that your dog cannot destroy. Do not use a tennis ball, as they are easily torn apart and eaten.

- For yarded dogs, get an old wheelbarrow tire and smear peanut butter inside it. Then leave it in the yard and watch your dog's joyous reaction. If you have a very large dog, use a car tire. You can also try a burlap sack smeared with lard or some other tasty substance.

- Leave a raw, un-cracked egg in his food bowl. He'll be puzzled at first, but will quickly solve the delicious puzzle. Don't worry about the raw egg; his digestive system is designed to deal with it.

- Freeze chunks of meat inside ice cubes and leave them in his food bowl. He'll excitedly lick and crunch at the cubes to get at the prize. You can also leave frozen meat broth cubes for him.

- For outdoor dogs (or for those owners willing to clean up the mess inside), get a large cardboard box, fill it with crumpled newspaper, and drop a few cookies into it. Leave the open box out for the dog to explore.

Social enrichments around the home Dogs greatly appreciate the company of people and other dogs. Unfortunately, they rarely get enough, and often end up isolated much of the day. This affects dogs detrimentally. Some forget how to act in social settings, and as a result can overreact with nervous excitement, jumping, or barking, or simply make a general nuisance out of themselves. Other isolated dogs can become suspicious and reserved; when strangers do come around, these dog hermits may hide, bark, or even growl or bite.

Enrichments around the home should include regular social visits. Natural owners know this, and as such provide meaningful social experiences for their dogs. They do not limit their dogs' contact to immediate family, as they know how important it is for a dog to accept the presence of friends and acquaintances outside of the "home pack." Friends of home children, relatives, neighbors—whoever steps through the front door with the blessings of the owner should be accepted by the dog.

A key to accomplishing this is the owner's ability to establish confident leadership. The owner must set an example for the dog to follow; when a dog sees his owner confidently greet guests, acceptance becomes much easier. Coddlers, lacking leadership status in their dogs' eyes, inadvertently leave their pets to decide if someone is acceptable or not. They lose the chance to set a competent example for their dog, which as a result often becomes nervous, pushy, vocal, or even aggressive upon a guest's arrival.

As a natural owner, make home life for your dog as socially rewarding as possible. The following social enrichments will do just that; try some or all of them!

- Pay unexpected visits home during the day. Try entering through the back door sometimes, if you have one. If you have time, give your dog a quick walk, or just play with him for a few minutes. He'll love the surprise!

- Schedule random visits to your home by neighbors, friends or paid dog walkers while you are gone. Start with people your dog knows and trusts, with you present. Once he accepts the new people, bow out. Then, gradually desensitize him to acquaintances and even friendly, capable strangers. Eventually, you can have these people work your dog's basic obedience, to generalize control over to other humans. Do not try this if your dog shows aggressive tendencies, or if he shows profound anxiety over others coming into your home or yard. For those dogs, schedule the visits only when you are home, and avoid having guests force themselves upon the dog. Just have them sit and read a book, wash dishes, or watch television while you go about your business. Eventually your dog will get used to the new presence.

- Have a well-behaved dog your own pet knows and likes visit your home for short, supervised visits. Let them play, then expect them to calm down and interact in a controlled, relaxed fashion. You can have them do "Down-Stays" in the living room, or graciously accept massages or brushing from you, one at a time.

- Have select, well-behaved, dog-savvy children over the age of twelve visit or take your dog for short walks. Doing so will help teach your dog to trust capable young persons. But, if your dog has a history of aggression or profound antisocial behavior, instead work your dog's obedience with a child or teen passively present. Have that child toss cookies to the dog whenever he performs properly.

- Expand your home territory to include a willing neighbor's home. Often the temporary change in venue will encourage shy dogs to come out of their shells. Only try this with neighbors your dog trusts. If he or she has a dog, be sure the dogs get along before trying this.

- Next time you have a party or meeting in the home, consider letting your dog stick around for a half-hour. Use the opportunity to work his manners and basic obedience. No jumping, begging or barking! Let guests reward him with treats in exchange for sitting or some other desirable learned behavior to teach tolerance and acceptance of strangers.

- Once your dog has reliable housetraining and admirable obedience and manners, consider getting another dog, preferably a puppy (if you have the time). Puppies are easier to train with an established canine role model in the home; your established dog will teach the youngster where and when to relieve itself, how to act, and what the rules are. In exchange for this mentoring, he will get a lifelong companion to keep him company, making your job a bit easier. If taking care of a puppy is too much work, you could try adopting an older dog with established housetraining and manners. Let your established dog meet and interact with any older dog first, to ensure they get along. Alternate gender; if you have a male, the new dog should be female, and vice versa. This decreases the odds of conflict. Or, consider fostering shelter dogs waiting for new homes!

Behavioral Enrichments

Any stimulating activities your dog participates in are considered behavioral enrichments. Rather than just altering your dog's home environment and then allowing your dog to react in a positive manner, behavioral enrichments require your dog to actively take part. These tap into your dog's need to explore, run, stalk, catch, and perform. As a natural owner, you should always afford your dog these opportunities.

The following are some excellent behavioral enrichments you can try with your dog. Give some a try; your dog will love the added activity.

Prey-driven enrichments When a dog fetches a ball or chases a cat, he shows his predatory drive to capture and covet "prey." A Black Lab retrieving ducks from a pond, the Collie herding sheep, the Greyhound chasing a mock rabbit around the track—these are all modifications of the canine drive to stalk and kill prey.

The canine prey drive, though closely related to the food drive, adds the passion of the stalk; it's "process" rather than "product" that truly excites the dog. That's why I have separated edible enrichments from prey-driven ones; the former involves simple eating, the latter, chasing, which is more fun, from the dog's perspective. Try the following:

- Fetch is the preeminent prey drive activity; your dog chases after the "prey," captures it, then brings it back to you in hopes that you will toss the ball out again and again. As described in Secret Four, teaching your dog to fetch a ball or toy will tap into his desire to chase, catch, and bring "prey" back to you, the leader.

- Some dogs go nuts for the light trail of a flashlight or laser pen. The erratic course of the bright point of light can send many dogs into hyper-chase mode; watching them go bonkers trying to capture the phantom can get hilarious! When using a laser pen, be sure not to shine the beam into anyone's eyes, as it can cause injury.

- **Operating a battery-operated, wind-up or remote-controlled toy around a driveway or basement floor for your dog to chase can be a fun way to stimulate his prey drive. Pet shops and mainstream toy stores often sell animated toys; try a few out and see how your dog reacts to them. Be sure not to leave your dog alone with one, though, as he might destroy or eat the toy. Another option is to use a toy that talks, barks, or meows!**

- **Some dogs respond to a teaser toy waved in their direction. A treat-filled ball on the end of a short rope and stick will inspire your dog, as will a dangled fake mouse dabbed with lavender oil or beef broth. As with any toy, don't let your dog have it for too long, as he may destroy or eat it. This type of enrichment works particularly well with terriers and toy dogs.**

The dog park Socializing with other dogs and persons at the dog park is a prime behavioral enrichment. In addition to sensory input, your dog gets to vie with other dogs for social position. This is good; he will learn where he stands among peers, and how to interact with dogs he has never met. You'll see a side of him rarely seen in the comfy confines of home, and may be surprised at what you discover about your little fur ball.

Before throwing him into the fray, you'll need to do some homework. First, visit the dog park without your dog to determine if it is appropriate. A fence tall enough to keep your dog in is essential. Next, check out the overall condition of the park; is it clean and free from potential danger? Do owners pick up after the dogs? As disease can be spread through contaminated feces, make sure the park is reasonably maintained.

Next, observe the dogs present. Are they huge unneutered bullies, or reasonable pets? Is any serious aggression occurring? Are the owners being attentive to their dogs, or ignoring the action? Are some dogs simply too threatening or rough? Use your instincts, and decide if your dog can handle the action; if not, find a more tranquil park.

Before taking your dog to an enclosed, off-leash dog park, it's a good idea to teach him to behave on leash, in your neighborhood and at public parks. Walking on a loose leash, greeting people and their dogs, and obeying basic commands outside are all prerequisites to going nose to nose with twenty other energy-charged pooches.

When you do take him to the dog park, choose a quiet time, with few dogs present. Walk him around the perimeter first, working his basic obedience. If other owners are coming or going with on-leash dogs, let yours greet them as a prelude to the free-for-all to come.

Then it's time to go for it. Bring him into the fenced enclosure and let him off the leash. Don't keep his leash on, as its restriction might cause your dog great anxiety, with all the others running free. Just let him loose and watch.

In the first minute he will be accosted by nearly every dog in the enclosure. They'll sniff at his rear, jump on him, chase him, lick at his mouth—all manner of posturing behavior. At first he'll be overwhelmed, and may growl or even snap. Or, he may simply take off running for joy. You won't know until you try it. Odds are any growling or nipping will ease off as soon as the others get used to the new guy; give it a few minutes, and don't interfere unless serious, "fangs-out" aggression erupts.

Once he gets used to it, let him play and posture long enough for him to be accepted. He may ignore you completely, or return to you from time to time for reassurance. Don't coddle him through it!

After ten minutes, call him to you and see if he'll come. If he does, praise him, but do not offer a treat, as this could spark aggression with the other dogs. Just pet and praise. If he doesn't come, calmly walk him down, clip on your leash, then take him out and work his obedience for a minute. Then let him back in and try the "Come Here" again. It's the absolute best laboratory in which to perfect this command.

Doggy day care Busy owners are turning to well-operated doggy day cares to care for their dogs during the long workday. Located in urban and suburban areas, these facilities take care of your dog's basic needs while also providing exercise and socialization, key enrichment goals. Dogs that experience separation anxiety while home alone are great candidates for day care, as are mischievous, homebound pooches that dig, bark or destroy.

The best day cares try to put your dog in with like-minded, similarly sized dogs. A frisky Jack Russell terrier, for instance, wouldn't be put into the same pen as a dog-aggressive Rottweiler. Instead, he'd be matched up with an appropriate playmate, perhaps another small breed with great social skills. Older dogs are either placed into a calmer pen with laid-back dogs, or given their own enclosure.

Many day care centers provide walking and playing options, as well as training, grooming and veterinary services. They'll feed your dog according to your requirements, and see to your pet's general welfare.

Don't just choose a doggy day care from the yellow pages. Visit the facility unannounced, to get a feel for the place. Is it clean-smelling and organized, or just someone's dank basement or yard? Do they offer the services you desire? Is there a veterinarian close by? Insist on a tour, and observe how diligent they are about pairing dogs up. Opt for a facility with enough employees to properly care for the dogs. If you see urine or feces everywhere, or barking dogs housed only in crates, take a pass. The key should be enrichment and competent care, and not simple convenience.

Make sure your dog is not overly coddled or spoiled at the doggy day care. Nothing is more frustrating than working for months on establishing a behavior change in your dog, only to have it sabotaged by a well-meaning but naïve kennel worker. For instance, if you have been training your dog to stay off of the sofa, but the day care has dog furniture he can climb up on, your efforts will be for naught. Be sure to explain any specific restrictions you have to the manager.

Keep Your Dog Healthy and Safe

Fat, Lazy and Vulnerable

The natural owner keeps his or her dog fit and protected. It's an essential responsibility that all effective owners appreciate and embrace. Unfortunately, this appreciation is too often neglected by many owners, to their dogs' disadvantage.

Back in the late nineties I wrote a book titled *Plump Pups and Fat Cats: A Seven-Point Weight Loss Program for Your Overweight Pet*. A diet book for pets? Yes, and with good cause. Today, millions of domestic pets are significantly overweight due to overfeeding and lack of exercise. Overweight dogs live shorter lives, and develop diseases and joint problems far sooner than do fit, active pets.

Don't blame natural owners for this; it's the fault of (you guessed it) coddlers, who spoil and bribe their dogs with gratis treats and excess food, and surrender to begging. Thinking that "food is love," the coddler tries to gain his or her dog's respect through food, and mistakes love for clever canine manipulation. The dog knows how easy it is to get a morsel; all it need do is sit pretty and whine a bit to win a tasty scrap. The dog trains the coddler to give up the goods.

In addition to overfeeding, owners of overweight dogs are also often guilty of under-exercising their pets. This makes sense; many who over-feed their dogs do so out of a sense of guilt over not spending enough time with their furry friends. Instead of going for a jog together, they toss Fluffy a cookie and go off to their own aerobics class. The cookie is an easy solution, and a cop-out.

Like humans, without the proper amount of activity a dog will eventually put on weight and lose aerobic capacity. Natural owners know this, and as such make sure their dogs get exercise on a daily basis. Remember, dogs need to have daily stimulation of body *and* *mind* to feel content.

Many owners also fail to adequately safeguard their dogs while in and around the home. It's easy to do, and not necessarily indicative of a bad owner. But the true natural owner, with his or her effective canine empathy "switched on," sees the home environment from a dog's perspective, and spots potential dangers the coddler does not. An exposed power cord, a shard of glass, an errant sewing needle, a faulty screen door, an antifreeze spill—natural owners see the dangers, and rid their homes of them.

The Elixir of Directed Exercise

Blessed with four legs, dogs were born to run. It's in their genes and bones; it's the running dream, the hunt, their raison d'etre, that mad dash to the lake, the sheer joy of a dog's days. They just plain love to move.

Even the smallest or oldest pooch needs to stretch his legs; as the leader, it's your job to make that happen. Exercise burns calories, strengthens the heart, and keeps joints and muscles resilient and strong. For dogs, it truly is the elixir of a long, healthy life.

Dogs don't know this. They think running, jumping, swimming, and romping is simply part and parcel of a good life, the thing to do when part of a happy, cohesive pack. They think it's an irresistibly fun way to be. As natural owners, we know it's good for them, and that it builds the dog/owner bond. Exercise promotes participation and measured competition, and helps dogs learn what their capabilities and limitations are. And, more important, it acts as a stress relief valve, minimizing nervous energy that can lead to destructive chewing, barking, or separation anxiety.

Getting enough exercise is hard enough for *us*; how can we see to it that our dogs get it too? Easy, by doing it together as often as possible, and by setting a schedule. Doing so creates a ritualistic tradition dogs learn to love. And you'll find yourself loving the experience too, as well as the opportunity to lose a few pounds in the process!

Before You Start

Let me list a few conditions before you begin, to ensure your dog stays happy and healthy:

- Avoid strenuous exercise until a dog is at least eight to twelve months of age. This will ensure that his evolving musculoskeletal system isn't overly stressed before it can handle the load. This means no hard running, and no leaping down from high spots. Also avoid jogs of over a mile, especially on pavement. With large breeds such as the Newfoundland, Great Dane, Mastiff or Rottweiler, wait until the dog is twelve to eighteen months of age before beginning any strenuous exercise. Though tough-looking, giant breeds experience rapid growth and impressive weight gains; this can stress joints more severely than in smaller breeds.

- Avoid yanking or twisting on a dog's legs during play, especially with young or petite pets, as this can cause severe joint trauma.

- Avoid exercising your dog right after a meal, as it can cause stomach upset, and in rare cases bloat, a life-threatening condition requiring immediate veterinary attention.

- Provide your dog with plenty of water after exercise. If the exercise session will last longer than thirty minutes, take water along with you. If in a hot climate, always take water along with you.

- If you intend to jog several miles each day on pavement, consider purchasing a set of doggy booties, to protect his pads. Also opt for the booties if you hike or jog in areas with cactus, sharp rocks, or the occasional shard of glass. The booties take getting used to; follow manufacturer's directions, and desensitize your dog to them slowly, while praising and rewarding.

- Avoid hazardous activities such as steep climbing, jogging off leash in high-traffic areas, swimming in deep, cold or swiftly-moving bodies of water, or heavy exercise when temperatures soar.

- Go easy with elderly dogs. Let them set the pace, and stop before they become winded or sore. Fit the activity to the dog's age—no agility classes or herding for geriatrics! And don't be too hard on little dogs, either; a Chihuahua won't tolerate a three-mile jog every day, or heavy exercise in extreme heat or cold. Settle for a brisk walk, and perhaps a round of fetch each day.

- Very heavy dogs and very small ones usually aren't strong swimmers; consider finding alternative exercises for them.

The Exercises

The following is a list of exercises and activities you can share with your dog. Choose any you like; just be sure to follow the above guidelines. And remember, if you are a natural, you'll participate for your own enjoyment!

Walks

A time-honored ritual of dog ownership, the daily walk is the most common way to exercise your dog and yourself. Covered in depth in Secret Four, the walk should take place at least once per day. Keep the pace brisk, stopping only when you decide your pooch needs a potty break. With healthy dogs, feel free to make it a half-hour or more. If your dog is very young or very old, limit brisk walking to fifteen minutes, or according to the dog's capabilities. Slower walks should be fine for these dogs provided no profound joint disorders are present.

Consider your dog's size; toy breeds or those with short legs may need a slower pace. Also, keep your dog's nails properly trimmed, as overly long nails alter the paw placement and put excess strain on his ankles. Lastly, be sure to carry a small plastic trash bag to pick up and discard any feces your dog may deposit along the way.

Jogging

A fabulous way to exercise your dog, jogging will also get you in great shape. Before beginning, make sure to follow these guidelines:

- Be sure your dog has great on-leash manners before jogging. He should know how to walk on a loose leash by your side, and understand that you are in charge, not him.

- Make sure your dog is wearing a proper ID tag in case he gets loose. Subcutaneous microchip ID is also a good idea; your veterinarian can insert one under your dog's skin, allowing other veterinarians or a pet shelter to read it and identify you as the owner.

- Attach a leash to your dog's regular collar or to a harness when jogging, not to a training collar. This will prevent choking should you trip or fall and drag the dog with you. Stay away from retractable leashes, as they encourage your dog to pull out and ignore you. When jogging, you want control and focus; retractables don't give this. A sturdy six-foot leash should be fine.

- Walk for a few minutes first before jogging, to warm up your dog's muscles and joints. This will help prevent injury, and will also give him the chance for a potty break before the jog.

- Never go for an off-leash jog, even if your dog walks nicely off-leash. You never know what unexpected incidents might occur that could spook your pet and cause injury, or worse.

- Your dog needs to feel at ease with the activity, so choose a quiet area without lots of cars, trucks, stray dogs, or excess noise. Once your dog gets used to jogging, you can explore busier areas, but to start, keep it simple and low key. For urbanites, choose early mornings or evenings, when activities diminish. Or, find a quiet, dog-friendly park.

- Be aware that other dogs might consider a running dog threatening. When you approach another owner walking his or her dog, slow down, confidently cross the street, wave hello and keep moving. Don't feel obliged to greet them; remember it is your jog, and your agenda.

- If a stray dog approaches aggressively, slow to a brisk walk and attempt to cross the street. Do not turn your back on the dog, and avoid sustained eye contact. Consider carrying a walking stick or pepper spray, which will dissuade most dogs from attacking. You can also use the handle end of your leash to whack a belligerent dog that gets too close, or even squirt him with your water bottle. Sometimes tossing a treat at the dog will distract him enough for you and your dog to get away unscathed. If the dog appears determined to attack, use your best judgment as to whether or not to unclip your dog's leash. Understand that your dog will stand a better chance of defending itself if untethered, even though it could mean temporarily losing him. If you have a small dog, though, picking him up may be the better option. Use any items that may be present—a belt, garbage can, rock, stick—anything that might fend off the attacker. Kick, scream, and call out for help. If you can, call 911 on your cell phone, or retreat into someone's yard. The bottom line is, as a natural owner, you must find a way to defend yourself and your dog; it's what a leader does.

- On warm days, jog in the early morning or evening. When cold, consider whether your dog can tolerate the frigid temperature. Lithe, short-coated breeds such as Whippets, Greyhounds, Vislas, Boxers and others may need a sweater on very cold days.

- On jogs lasting more than fifteen minutes, take water. Keep a filled bottle and a collapsible cup in a fanny pack, and give Fluffy a drink at the turn.

- Wear reflective clothing if jogging in the evening or night-time. You can even purchase a reflective vest for your dog!

- Avoid jogging with your dog right after he has eaten, as this can cause stomach upset or even life-threatening bloat. Wait two hours to be safe.

- If jogging with a baby stroller, never attach the leash to the stroller. If your dog panics or takes off, he could topple or drag the stroller, and hurt your child. Instead, keep the leash in your hand.

Hiking

For those fond of hiking, consider taking your dog along with you next time, provided the trail allows dogs. The chance to be out in nature will stimulate his senses and work his muscles like few other activities can. The experience will also allow you to see his canine instincts fully engaged; he'll be smelling raccoon, deer, possum, and every other animal and person that has been down the path in the last week!

Check regulations for the venue; most hiking areas require dogs to be leashed, for everyone's safety. Consider using a long lead (eight to twelve feet), to give your dog a chance to explore a bit. If off-leash activity is allowed, be sure your dog is well trained before allowing it. A reliable recall command is mandatory for off-leash hiking!

While hiking, don't require your dog to walk by your side. This is one time that he can enjoy sniffing and exploring. As long as he doesn't yank you around or get tangled, let him have fun. Afterward, go back to a more controlled walking posture.

Bear, wolf, snake, coyote, porcupine, raccoon—all can harm even the strongest of dogs. Even spiders or scorpions can be fatal, especially to small pets. Also watch for precipitous drops, fast-moving water, caves, melting ice bridges or other natural dangers, to prevent your pooch from having a severe accident.

When hiking or camping with your dog, take water and food to last. Check him for ticks, fleas and other parasites, during and after. Burrs, spines, thorns, poison ivy and other irritants can make your dog miserable, so check his paws, face and coat often.

If you choose a rugged area or a desert terrain with cactus, purchase a set of doggy booties at your local pet store. You'll need to condition him to the booties beforehand, according to the manufacturer's directions.

Discourage your dog from drinking from streams, ponds or lakes, as these often contain giardia or other harmful parasites. Also make sure he doesn't consume any dead animals, as they could make him ill, or infect him with parasites.

Biking

Those who want to combine exercising their dogs with bike riding can do so, provided proper precautions are taken. I'd advise against simply tying your dog's leash to your bike, as the leash can easily tangle in the gears or chain, resulting in a nasty spill. You also never want to hold the leash while riding, as this would restrict your ability to control the bike.

The best way to run your dog beside your bike is to purchase a commercial product designed to make it safe. Most are designed with a spring-loaded plastic or metal bar mounted perpendicular to the bike frame and extending out a few feet to the right; a short lead is attached to this, then clipped to a harness the dog wears. The dog is positioned on the right side, away from traffic and far enough from the bike to maintain balance and security. These devices are available at pet stores or from online providers; just type "dog" and "bicycle" into your search engine for numerous examples.

Using one of these products will require you to train your dog to the new behavior. He may at first get confused at being on your right side; with practice, though, he'll learn to adapt. It's vital that you begin using the product in an area free from distractions and traffic; a vacant parking lot is perfect. Start out slow and short, and be positive. Consider taking a second person along to jog on the dog's right side, to give him the impression that he is simply on a jog, only with you beside him on a bike.

At first, travel in a straight line, varying speed from a crawl to perhaps five miles per hour. Then incorporate gradual turns, starting with slight ones to the left. The bar extension and short lead will gradually pull on his harness, inciting him to turn. Then try gradual right turns; the bar and short lead will again compel him to turn in that direction. This is another reason for using the rigid bar instead of a leash.

Limit this activity to dogs that can keep up a pace of ten miles per hour for extended periods. This means medium to large-sized breeds in excellent health. Small, obese or elderly dogs should take a pass on this one!

Choose quiet areas with low traffic flow. Wear a helmet, and take along water. Be sure that he is up to the high level of exercise.

Swimming

Swimming works every muscle in the body without the stress on joints that running produces. It's also a great enrichment activity, and a way to build confidence.

Though most dogs like to play in the water, many never quite learn to swim confidently. To do so, follow these steps:

- **With puppies or small dogs, start out with a kiddy pool. Toss in a toy, and climb in yourself. With adolescent or adult dogs, choose a body of water without much current or wave action. Bring a toy, and get in yourself. The more people and dogs you bring in, the better; if your dog sees everyone having fun, he'll be more likely to relax and go for it.**

- **Never throw the dog into the water. Take your time, and gradually increase the depth. Let the experience build confidence up, not tear it down.**

- **With toy dogs, heavy-boned breeds and older dogs, use a doggy life jacket. If at the ocean or a fast-moving stream or river, use the life jacket for any dog (at least in the beginning), and be sure to determine if your dog can handle the current. If in doubt, choose a calmer body of water.**

- **If using a pool, make sure there are steps the dog can use to get in and out. If he tires or gets worried, get him out.**

- **When swimming from a boat, use the life jacket, and be sure to help the dog back into the boat.**

Treadmills

For active dogs that might go stir-crazy during a cold or rainy winter, a treadmill might be just the thing. Older dogs in need of regular, moderate exercise can also benefit from workouts on a treadmill, to keep joints supple and muscles strong.

Electric treadmills are better than self-propelled models, because the speed and action of the unit are more consistent, and independent of the dog's input. A large dog's stride is often longer than that of a human's; be sure to take this into consideration when purchasing. Opt for one with adjustable incline as well, for a complete workout.

Supervise your dog when he is on a treadmill; *never* tie off his leash and leave him! Also, make sure the leash never gets caught in the mechanism.

You can't throw your pooch onto a treadmill and expect him to take to it instantly. Instead, you'll need to condition him to it. Here's how:

- **Place the treadmill in a spot that allows you to approach it at any angle.**

- **Let the dog get used to its presence. Place treats onto the treadmill throughout the day, and encourage him to step up onto it to eat them. Praise whenever he does! Then, for a few days, feed him his dinner atop the treadmill. Doing so will desensitize him to the unit.**

- **Next, train him to stand on the treadmill with you crouching out front with cheese in your hand. Let him nibble the cheese for a bit before releasing it, to extend the time he stands in the desired position. Praise and say "Good Stand!" Do this often for several days before moving on.**

- With your dog standing on the treadmill and you out in front holding his leash, have someone turn the unit on the slowest speed possible, on a flat incline. Hold the leash and praise; he will probably begin taking steps without even realizing it. If he does, praise, but avoid giving a treat at this stage, as he is just learning to get his "sea legs."

- If he jumps off, shut it down and reposition him into a stand. Reward with a treat and try again. Once he'll walk at the slowest speed, slowly increase speed to a desirable pace. This could take a week, so be patient. Continue to stand in front, holding the leash. Praise!

Eventually you will be able to leave the dog's leash off, and even sit in a chair nearby while he gets a good workout. Just be sure to never leave him alone, or tie off the leash.

Stairs and Hills

A simple way to get your dog in great aerobic shape is to run him up and down a few flights of stairs, or a grassy hill. You can accompany him, train him to do it alone, or use the help of a friend to "tag team" him back and forth, up and down.

Choose this exercise only with dogs in excellent shape, with no signs of heart or joint disease. Don't try it with dogs under a year of age, either, as the stress could adversely affect developing joints. With giant breeds such as the Mastiff, Great Dane or Rottweiler, wait until the dog is eighteen months of age before running him up and down stairs or hills.

Hide-and-Seek

A good game of hide-and-seek is a fun way for both of you to get exercise. If your dog isn't reliable off leash, limit it to indoor or fenced-in areas. Off-leash competence makes it more fun; you can take your dog to a wooded area and have a ball.

At first, take a friend to help. Have him or her hold your dog's collar while you take off and hide behind a tree, rock, or structure; then the dog is released with a "Find Him!" command, and the game is on. As your scent is etched into his psyche, he will no doubt find you very quickly!

Slowly increase the distance your dog must search to find you. Then, instead of using a friend's help, teach your dog to hold a "Sit" while you hide. Remember to say *"Sit"* then *"Wait,"* not *"Stay,"* as "Stay" is a permanent position that can only be released with a touch. "Wait" is a temporary command that can be ended by you with a verbal command from a distance.

Tag

Tag can be loads of fun. Played in a yard or fenced area, the objective is not to chase your dog (a leadership faux pas), but to tag him on the rear end as he tries to run by you. After getting him excited to run around, simply tag him as he tries to slip by. Don't chase him, as you'll lose every time, unless he's a three-legged fifteen-year-old.

Include friends in the game; just make sure the space used is large enough to allow a good workout, but small enough for you to succeed in tagging him. End while he is still excited to continue, and be sure to give him a nice treat or toy reward.

Draft Work

A few years ago, while visiting a vacant soccer field to let my dog stretch his legs, I eyed a ruddy old man and a gigantic Malamute in the middle of the field. The dog had a padded harness on; attached to it were two chains leading back to a tractor tire; the dog was happily dragging the big tire up and down the field!

While he and the dog took a break, we spoke. He'd lived in Alaska for years and always had Malamutes, a huge Arctic breed traditionally used to pull sleds or carts, or to do all manner of draft, or pulling work. His dogs loved dragging heavy things around; indeed, this tire must have weighed three hundred pounds! I didn't ask how he got the tire back into the bed of his pickup; I half-wondered if he'd trained the dog to do that, too.

Owners of strong breeds can join dog "carting" or "drafting" clubs, which train dogs to pull carts, wagons, sleds, or heavy objects. Located in many countries, competitions test a dog's strength and endurance; some giant breeds are uncanny in their abilities to pull heavy weights, in some cases dragging thousands of pounds!

If you have a strong breed-type such as a Saint Bernard, Rottweiler, Mastiff, Malamute, Siberian Husky, Newfoundland, German Shepherd, pit bull or Bernese Mountain Dog, consider finding a canine drafting club in your area. These dogs (especially the Rottweiler, Malamute, Husky, Mastiff and Saint Bernard) were used throughout history as draft animals; indeed, cultures such as the Inuit still depend on dogs to pull loads of equipment and supplies.

Though I personally frown upon extreme sledding competitions that risk a dog's life, I see nothing wrong with teaching your big dog to pull a small cart or weight. It's great for strength training and cardiovascular health, provided the dog is in great shape.

Drafting requires a padded harness for your dog, and some sort of cart, wagon, or heavy object (such as a tire or log). After desensitizing your dog to the harness, the goal is to attach him to the desired load and have him pull it for a prescribed distance.

I'd strongly recommend contacting a dog drafting/carting organization in your area before trying this; you'll find many listed online. They can train you and your dog properly, and show you where to find the proper equipment.

Additional Fun Activities

As long as you do not endanger your dog's life, nearly any activity is fair game. Covered in detail in Secret Seven: Endow your Dog with Purpose, the following activities are great ways to exercise your dog:

- **Agility classes and competitions: This group activity will get your dog moving and thinking.**
- **Dog parks: Your dog will run, play and socialize to his heart's content.**

- **Fetch:** The time-honored standard, playing fetch will burn calories and build the recall command.

- **Flying disk activities:** Like fetch, your dog will stay in shape catching and retrieving a disk.

- **Flyball:** This organized relay race will tone your dog's muscles and build his competitive spirit.

- **Herding:** No other exercise will build strength and stamina like this instinctive activity.

- **Recall:** Having your dog run back and forth between two persons will build vigor and obedience.

- **Tracking:** Teaching your pooch to track objects and persons will work his muscles and nose.

Diet: Fuel for a Natural Relationship

The alpha wolf rules the roost in part because of his uncanny ability to track and stalk prey, then choreograph the kill. The passion and camaraderie a successful hunt evokes within the canine heart can never be underestimated.

One of the perks of domestication is that your dog need not hunt down his food (though some do try, to the dismay of cats and squirrels). As his natural owner, you provide him with the nutrition he needs to stay healthy and sated throughout his life. Quite a deal for him; all he need do in return is provide you with what all dogs should; love and obedience, manners, a modicum of protection, and lots of fun.

No longer allowed to fend for himself, your pooch must depend on you for food. This dependence is a great lever, and an important tool in managing the relationship properly. Remember that the passion for the hunt still lives in your dog's heart; it needs to be tapped and directed for you to maintain a genuine sense of leadership and control.

Your dog's diet directly affects his health and behavior. Malnourished dogs live shorter lives and contract diseases and infections more readily. Every system in the body suffers, including the dog's ability to think rationally. He'll be weaker, slower, sicker and less developed than other dogs, and far less happy. Indeed, his moods and manners will suffer, not only from a lack of nutrients, but also from the insecurity borne of poor leadership. After all, what kind of owner fails to properly feed his or her dog?

Food Is a Tool

Food defines you as the great provider, giving you a key tool in modifying behavior. Who hasn't used a treat to get a dog to sit? When done right, the act of feeding your dog solidifies your authority; done badly, though, it can hurt your reputation and cause problems. For instance, the coddler who placates a begging dog at the dinner table teaches that dog to be dominant, and eventually obese. The owner who only gives treats in exchange for some desirable behavior such as "Sit" motivates his or her dog, and clearly establishes who is in charge.

Feeding time is a great time to teach. Few motivators work as effectively as food; you'll have your dog's undivided attention at that moment, so why not take advantage of it? I always ask my dogs to do something for their suppers; a sit, speak, spin—some little thing to teach that all good things must be earned. At least make sure your dog acts in a civil, polite manner when dinner is about to be served.

Dietary Needs of the Dog

Though not pure carnivores like cats, canines come much closer to it than we do. If we look to wolves again, we see their diet consists mainly of muscle and organ meats, sinew and bone (including the nutrient-rich marrow). They also derive nutrients from consuming the prey animal's predigested stomach and intestinal contents. Dogs graze on plant material, too, though this is often for purgative reasons. As a rule, though, wolves process all they need from meat and bones.

Dogs share the same dietary needs. Look at their teeth; designed to grasp, shear, shred and crush, they are perfect tools for a canine's dietary needs. The dog's large mouth is designed not for endless chewing, but for swallowing hunks of meat quickly, which are quickly digested by acids more potent than our own. Meat and bones get broken down and absorbed quickly, to allow the dog to be up and running again quickly.

Unlike humans, dogs lack a special enzyme in their saliva. Called *amylase*, it helps us begin the digestion of carbohydrates. Dogs do not have amylase because they do not ingest raw carbohydrates in bulk. In fact, dogs that eat too many carbohydrates tend to pass them through the digestive tract undigested; it's why dogs fed inexpensive, high-carbohydrate supermarket kibble pass larger stools than dogs fed a meat-based diet.

Dogs need 18-25 percent of their diet to be protein and 10–15 percent to be fat. The remainder consists of moisture, fiber, carbohydrates, vitamins, minerals and other supplements. Puppies and pregnant bitches need higher protein and fat percentages as well as more calcium and phosphorus, while older dogs need less. These numbers can vary considerably, however; only you and your veterinarian can make the right choice.

Food Choices

I divide an owner's choice of food into several categories. Let's look at each and then decide what is best for your dog:

Premium commercial foods Dogs once ate the remains of a human family's meal. For the last fifty years, however, owners have had commercial dog foods available for purchase. Sold in bags or cans, these foods are designed to supply a dog with the nutrients needed for basic health.

Up until the last fifteen years or so, commercial dog foods were notorious for containing sub-par ingredients, including "meat by-products," a term that encompasses anything from hooves and fur to feathers, rancid meat, or even rat droppings. Loaded with cereals, hulls, low-grade meats and risky preservatives, these foods were a step down from feeding human leftovers. Their only advantages were convenience and price.

Today, premium commercial dog foods are vastly improved. Pet stores stock quality dry or canned foods that supply dogs with what they need to stay healthy. Despite what some say about the "evils" of commercially available foods, I believe carefully formulated, premium-priced offerings provide most dogs with a diet capable of maintaining good health and long life. They use human-grade meat as the primary ingredient, add cooked whole grains such as rice or barley, and add only natural preservatives. Formulated by nutritionists, they include all needed vitamins and minerals.

Not too long ago, many quality pet foods became tainted with toxins tracked to shipments of Chinese wheat. Hundreds of dogs and cats worldwide died of renal failure because of this. To my mind, the main culprit is the pet food industry's contracting out the manufacture and packaging of their products to third party companies who, though diligent in their adherence to formula, procured their own ingredients—including wheat products from overseas.

I have since decided to purchase pet food products formulated and manufactured by only one company, and packaged either by them or by a third party carefully monitored by the manufacturer. I will not purchase any foods containing overseas ingredients, as these cannot be monitored by the FDA or any other regulating body. Finding a company that fits these parameters was not easy; I had to really do my homework. But if you make the proper enquiries to the customer service staff at each food company, you will be able to determine which make their own foods, and which refuse to use overseas ingredients. Doing so may save your pet's life!

Supermarket dog foods Beware of most dog foods sold in supermarkets, especially the inexpensive brands. Though these too have improved dramatically in quality over the last decade, most do not compare well with top-of-the-line premium pet store dog foods.

Supermarket dog foods are often formulated with grains as the predominant ingredient instead of meat. The meat contained is often listed as "meat by-products," meaning poor quality. In fact, much of this "meat" isn't even human grade. The fats contained are often restaurant greases or low-grade rendered fats that offer little in the way of nutrition. Personally, I wouldn't give it to my dog.

Most also use potentially harmful chemical preservatives such as ethoxyquin, BHA and BHT to increase shelf life. Better dog foods are preserved with natural ingredients such as Vitamins E or C, clove or rosemary oil, which, though not as effective as the chemical preservatives, will keep the dog food fresh for several months.

I don't recommend supermarket dog foods for your dog, unless finances demand it. Better to spend the extra twenty dollars per month for the premium pet store varieties.

Canned versus dry Premium canned dog foods found in pet stores are formulated with the same care as premium dry foods. They do differ in several ways, however. First, they have a much higher moisture content, approaching 60 percent or more. Though water is good for your dog, this makes it necessary to feed more of it to your pet than the dry version. Canned food is therefore more expensive per feeding, so serving it exclusively will probably double your expenses. Canned will keep almost indefinitely though, while dry food lasts only three to four months. Canned will also promote tartar on your dog's teeth more readily than dry food. Lastly, dogs fed on canned only will often turn their noses up if you try to switch them over to dry. I suppose I would too!

The same care in the selection of dry food should be given to canned. Use only foods formulated and manufactured by your pet food's parent company, and avoid any unmonitored overseas ingredients.

A good compromise for variety is to feed a mix of dry and canned food. This makes the dry food more palatable, and increases the water content and the amount of meat the dog eats.

A natural diet More concerned dog owners have switched their pets over to a natural, or raw food diet, consisting of raw or very lightly cooked meats, cooked whole grains and vegetables, and vitamin/mineral supplements. More closely mirroring the wild canine's diet, if properly formulated it is in my opinion the best diet for a dog.

Owners feeding this diet grind together fresh muscle and organ meats, chicken or turkey necks, and some well-cooked grains and vegetables. Some first lightly cook or microwave the meat to kill potential parasites and surface bacteria; though many claim this is unnecessary, I believe a quick dunk into boiling water is a good idea. After blending the mix, a sprinkle of a vitamin/mineral supplement can be added. This natural blend can then either be fed to the dog in the proper amounts, or frozen, where it will keep for months.

The problem with feeding a raw natural diet to your dog lies in its formulation. Some well-meaning owners inadvertently end up creating a home-cooked food deficient in certain essential nutrients, or get the percentages of protein, fat and carbohydrates wrong. Over time, this can harm your dog. Calorie counts can also be off, as raw foods generally contain less calories pound-for-pound than do kibble. This can result in an underweight pet, or one that is constantly begging for more food.

Preparation time can be a deciding factor in feeding your dog a raw diet. With kibble, you simply scoop and serve; the most work you'll do is perhaps soak the food in warm water for a few minutes, or add a few spoons of premium canned food to it. With a raw diet, you must do the proper nutritional research, shop for ingredients, prepare the food, thaw if need be, and find space to store it. For busy people with little time to cook even for themselves, this can be a challenge.

The other issue is price. If you decide to feed your pooch a raw diet, expect your dog food bill to double or triple, compared to a premium dry food. Though buying in bulk and having ample freezer space cuts the expense, it will still be more expensive than kibble or canned. You will also need a meat grinder, cost-prohibitive for some owners.

Many will still opt for the raw diet, while others will find the cost excessive, especially those with multi-dog families. My advice is this: if you can afford it, give it a try. But if it proves too expensive or time-consuming, don't feel guilty over feeding a dog premium dry or canned food. Your dog will still live a healthy life.

I include a home-cooked natural dog food recipe at the end of
this section. If you follow it closely, you shouldn't have a problem
with formulation.

A healthy compromise A great compromise for those worried about
price or preparation time is combining the best of both worlds. I'm not
ashamed to admit that I do this with my dogs. I select a top-notch dry
food (mine is an adult lamb-and-rice formula formulated and manufactured by the parent company) and supplement it with regular feedings
of lightly-cooked foods. Chicken or turkey necks, lamb, chicken or beef
muscle meat, chicken or beef liver, raw eggs, cottage cheese, the occasional knuckle bone—whatever I think will be a healthy addition is
added to the menu. I reduce the amount of kibble accordingly, and
always let the kibble soak in a cup or two of warm water for ten minutes
before serving. This ensures proper moisture content, increases the
apparent volume without increasing calories, and reduces the chance
of bloat. Often I forego the kibble entirely and simply give my dogs an
"all-natural" evening.

This strategy has worked for me. None of my dogs have ever suffered
kidney or liver disease or shown food-allergic symptoms. In fact, my
dog Louie, a Rottweiler/Shepherd mix, lived to the ripe age of sixteen,
unheard of for his breed profile. He ate the above-mentioned diet nearly
all his life, a testament to its nutritional worth.

If price and time are an issue, consider this feeding technique. Start
out slowly by adding a chicken neck every other day. Don't worry about
the bones; neck vertebrae never splinter. Also try adding some chicken
or beef liver, a raw egg, or even a can of sardines. Experiment, and feel
free to blanch or microwave something if you wish, as doing so will not
appreciably reduce the nutritional value.

Supplements If you feed your dog a balanced diet, the need for supplements becomes minimal. But if you're concerned that your dog might
not be getting all the vitamins or minerals he needs, feel free to give him
a daily vitamin/mineral supplement. For those feeding an all-raw diet,

this becomes a priority, to cover any nutrients that might be missing in your homemade blend. Available at any pet store, choose the chewable form, much easier than stuffing a pill down your dog's throat. You can also get the powdered form and sprinkle it on his food. I use chewables, and use them for training.

Some owners sprinkle a small amount of bone meal onto their dogs' food, for calcium. A teaspoon is fine if you like. I feed my dogs chicken necks, sardines, raw eggs still in the shell, an occasional knuckle bone, and a premium kibble, all of which contain calcium. Because of this I forego the bone meal.

I also add olive or flaxseed oil to my dog's food, or an occasional salmon skin (left over from my dinner). This ensures the proper amounts of Omega 3 and Omega 6 oils. Don't add too much, as you could encourage diarrhea. Half a teaspoon is fine.

Do not over-supplement your dog's food; some are simply unnecessary expenses that appeal to our "human" side. If you have any concerns, ask your trusty veterinarian.

Plump Pups

When I see a client's dog for the first time, the pet's weight is often a great first indicator of the owner's competence. A fat dog usually means an untrained, pushy pet with poor obedience training and an indulgent owner. A trim dog more often points to a well-fed and exercised pet, with a natural owner at the helm.

Deciding how much to feed a dog is largely trial-and-error. Though pet food manufacturers give suggested amounts according to a dog's body weight, I have found these to be exaggerated. For instance, one of my dogs, a lanky five-year-old shepherd/retriever mix named Flavio (he thinks he is a race car driver), maintains his athletic physique on two to three cups of food per day, including raw offerings. He gets treats too, and an occasional salmon skin. If I followed feeding directions on the average dog food bag, he'd be eating around four cups of kibble per day, enough to cause fairly rapid weight gain. I'd have to run him five miles per day to keep the weight off.

Feel your dog's ribcage. You should just barely feel his ribs beneath a thin layer of muscle, fat and skin. If you cannot discern the location of each rib, he is overweight. If his ribs are plainly visible through his skin, then you need to up his food; otherwise, go for a trim look—the ribcage should have nice girth, with a smooth, tapered narrowing to the groin. If the line from the bottom of the ribcage to the groin appears more parallel to the floor than tapered, your dog may be overweight.

Take a look at your dog from above; the same gradual taper should be evident from the ribs to the hindquarters. If you see an abrupt, right-angle "tuck" where the rear-most ribs end, your dog may be under-weight. If the line from the rear ribs to the hindquarters has no inward taper at all, he's probably chubby. If you go for a nice taper with just a hint of rib, your dog will be just fine.

Weigh your dog. If small enough, you can hold him, weigh both of you, then weigh yourself and subtract. If too large for this, take him to your veterinarian, who will be happy to weigh him. Discuss your dog's weight with your veterinarian; he or she can tell in a second if your pal is "poochy."

If your dog is overweight, reduce food by about 20 percent, while perhaps increasing exercise. Weigh him each week and watch the weight come off.

Your dog cannot cook, or open the fridge. You are completely respon-sible for his weight, so take charge! Limit treats with an overweight dog, too; reduce their size and frequency, and absolutely no begging!

One last point; do not free-feed, or leave food down all day. Most free-feeders "snack" all day and end up pudgy. Owners rarely keep track of the food, and replenish the bowl's contents too often. Feed once or twice per day, and measure the amounts!

Feeding Multiple Dogs

If you have several dogs in the home, you probably know where each is in the pecking order. You can tell by behavior; one rolls over and exposes his belly, or licks at the dominant dog's face. The "boss" dog gets to toys and chews faster, then dominates them. The dominant dog comes and goes first, and monopolizes greeting rituals with other people and dogs. The subordinate pretty much lets the dominant dog call the shots.

Don't allow this at dinnertime. If permitted, the dominant dog will eat the submissive's food as well as his own. One dog will get fat while the other gets bony. A primary observation in two-dog homes is that fat dogs are nearly *always* dominant.

Monitor your dogs at dinnertime, and never allow theft. If necessary, feed them in separate rooms or crates. Remember that *you* direct the feeding ritual. Even though one dog will naturally dominate the other, both must be able to eat undisturbed!

Food Aggression

An indication of a coddler's home occurs when a dog shows aggression when a human attempts to touch his bowl, treats, chews or toys. Let this go on and the relationship becomes an unnatural, dysfunctional mess.

If you have this problem, you need to turn it around without undue conflict or risk. The solution, beyond reestablishing yourself as the leader (see Secret Two) is to, for several weeks, ensure that *every morsel of food your dog eats* comes from your hand. Without a bowl to guard, he will have to change his pushy ways to get that meal.

Here's what to do:

Remove the food bowl. At dinnertime, place the dog's normal amount of food into a different bowl, then, while holding it in your hand, feed your dog the food, handful by handful, until he is done. Be sure to make him sit for every morsel! Though this will take awhile, it is essential.

After a week, place a handful of food into the bowl, ask him to sit, then place the bowl down onto the floor and let him eat. Now pick up the empty bowl, place another handful into it, ask him to sit, then place the bowl down. Continue this

until the entire dinner is eaten. This will recondition him to accept the bowl handling. The power of food returns to you!

After a week of this, leave the bowl on the floor and simply place handfuls of food into it, allowing him to eat. Randomly pick the bowl up to show that you are in charge. Eventually he will see that you touching the bowl means food is coming. Continue this step for two weeks.

Now separate your dog's meal into two parts and deliver each part to the bowl, using the same technique. While he eats, randomly pick up the bowl and place a piece of cheese into it.

Now place your dog's entire meal into the bowl. Make him sit, then put the bowl down. After ten seconds, pick up the bowl. Intermittently place a piece of cheese into it, then place it back down. Repeat this two or three times. If he shows any aggression at this point, go back to step two for two weeks. He will eventually understand that you touching the bowl means good things are on the way! If he does not respond in this way, seek out a trained pet behaviorist.

A Simple Home-Cooked Recipe for Your Dog

You can feed this recipe to your dog exclusively, or use it in smaller quantities as a supplement to his normal food. Each cup contains about 250 calories.

The average fifteen-pound dog will need between 400–750 calories per day; the average forty-pound dog between 700–1000; the average seventy-pound dog between 1000–1400. These are broad approximations; younger dogs will need more, older dogs less. Very active dogs will also need more, while sedentary pets will require less. Use trial-and-error to determine what's right for your dog.

NATURAL DIET RECIPE

2 cups raw or lightly-cooked muscle meat (beef, chicken, lamb, turkey or fish, no pork)

1 cup raw or lightly-cooked organ meat (liver, heart, kidney, lung or gizzard, again no pork)

1 raw or lightly-cooked turkey neck or 2 chicken necks

2 cups well-cooked whole grains (brown rice, barley or oats)

1 cup well-cooked, chopped vegetables (green beans, broccoli, zucchini or carrots)

1 raw egg

1 teaspoon olive, fish or flaxseed oil

Grind all the meat together. Mix in the other ingredients then let sit for fifteen minutes. Yields about seven to eight cups. Can be frozen and stored for several months. Feed according to caloric guidelines listed.

Veterinary Support: The Essential Safety Net

Great veterinarians don't just administer vaccinations or treat existing problems; they play the role of medical detective, looking for subtle signs of oncoming illness or disease that, if caught early, can be effectively managed or eliminated. Great vets practice preventive health care, making sure all judicious vaccinations are given, and that your dog's diet provides him with the right nutrients. They clean teeth, tend to parasitic infestations, and even scrutinize coat and skin condition for signs of possible illness.

Veterinarians can help with behavioral issues, particularly those caused by a medical problem. They can suggest solutions to house-training woes, and even counsel you on grooming techniques. And when a trainer or pet behaviorist is needed, your veterinarian can often provide a referral.

Most of all, your vet will be there for you in times of emergency. Should an accident or dire medical situation require life-saving treatment or surgery, he or she can perform the procedure or refer you to the proper specialist.

Effective canine empathy means being aware of your dog's day-to-day health and disposition. When alerted to a possible problem, the natural owner understands the vital role a veterinarian plays in the health of his or her dog.

Less attentive owners wait until serious symptoms surface before scheduling a visit. Still others make an appointment only when vaccinations are due, or when infestations make home life unbearable. They go to their own doctors once each year for a preventive check-up; why deny dogs the same courtesy?

At your dog's yearly exam, your vet will weigh your dog, give him a nose-to-tail physical exam, and check vital signs for anything abnormal. He or she will also probably perform several tests, including:

Blood Test, to check for:

Red and white cell count, indicative of possible anemia or infection

Hemoglobin assessment, to determine if enough oxygen is being delivered to the cells

Platelet count, to assess clotting ability

Blood glucose, indicative of diabetes (excess glucose) or hypoglycemia (insufficient glucose)

Excess amounts of waste materials and other substances, indicative of liver or kidney failure

Urinalysis, to check for:

Blood in the urine, indicative of infection, or bladder or kidney disease

Excess sugar, a possible sign of diabetes

Excess proteins, a sign of possible organ disease

Urine concentration, an indicator of dehydration

Any infection or infestation

Fecal Test, to check for:

Parasitic infection

Gastrointestinal disease

Any necessary vaccinations will be given, as well as treatments such as flea-and-tick preventive or de-worming medication. If necessary, X-rays or ultrasound can diagnose broken bones or other internal problems. Even your dog's teeth and gums will be examined for problems.

If all goes well, your dog will get a clean bill of health. If not, you're in the right place to get help.

When to Take Your Dog to the Veterinarian

Be aware of your dog's appearance and behavior. Unusual symptoms should prompt you to make an appointment with your veterinarian; these include:

Coughing or sneezing

Shivering, drooling, panting or excess vocalization

Excess scratching

Altered sleep patterns, or hiding

Dramatic change in appetite, thirst or elimination habits

Persistent head shaking

Lethargy or hyperactivity

Lameness

Greasy coat or hair loss

Uncharacteristic aggression

Excess discharges

Rashes or sores

Uncharacteristic odor

Pale gums

Discomfort to the touch

Loss of balance

Remember; you can't do it all. By taking your dog to the veterinarian once per year, you'll ensure the optimal health of your friend. It's what a natural leader would do!

Enlightened Supervision

The natural owner supervises his or her dog with confidence, poise and perception, without resorting to overprotection or emotional extremes. That means no outbursts unless absolutely necessary, and, perhaps as important, no unearned fawning or coddling. You should present yourself in an even, supportive, authoritative manner, and avoid unpredictable or unnecessary emotion.

Picture yourself as an alpha wolf. In all likelihood, you would not only be the CEO, but also the parent to the younger canines in the group. You are a role model, a protector, a teacher. You know that your ultimate goal, beyond the survival of the pack, is to foster autonomy and cooperation, and an ability to carry on the line of succession.

How does a pack leader do these things? Not by doting, or by seeing to it that every subordinate is perfectly content. A leader who spends too much time fussing over others will lose his or her leadership status and erode pack confidence. So too will a leader who bullies, or rules by fear instead of example. No; a true leader protects, but lets reasonable "stressors" affect a subordinate dog enough to build confidence and character.

When you supervise your dog, do so *proactively*, not reactively. Instead of waiting for problems to surface, catch them in their infancy; see as a dog would see, and grasp how a developing circumstance might slowly affect your dog's psyche, leading to a behavioral problem. For instance, if your neighbor brings home a new dog and puts it in his or her yard, realize that your dog will smell its presence even before seeing the animal. This could lead to a sudden desire by him to dig under or jump over the fence, or at the very least show an increased incidence of barking, marking or fence fighting. To deal with this issue, you should:

- **Reevaluate your fence security**

- **Let the dogs meet on neutral territory, to defuse territorial issues that could lead to fence-fighting**

- **Have your dog spend less time loose in your yard**

- **Invite the other dog over for structured play sessions**

Part of supervising your dog should include sensing territorial problems as they occur, then correcting them. For instance, a screen door with a torn screen or faulty latch can lead to an escaped dog; it's best to fix it immediately. Or, if your children leave doors or windows open, you'll need to address the issue promptly, to avoid catastrophe.

The same goes for dangerous objects left about the home, things we take for granted. These include pins, garbage, rubber bands, marbles, nails, nuts, bolts and screws, wiring, medications, spray cleaners, or anything that a dog could get into.

Remember; see things from a dog's-eye view. Realize how tasty (and deadly) antifreeze is to a dog. Understand how scent-rich the TV remote control is, and how likely it would be for a puppy or young dog to crunch into it. See how tempting and potentially deadly an old VCR tape could be if your dog broke it open and started slurping the tape down like spaghetti. You need to be vigilant, and protective.

Don't let your concerns turn you into a nervous Nellie. In your dog's eyes you should appear cool, capable, and sincere; showing stress or acting like a pandering fussbudget tells your dog the exact opposite. He sees *and smells* you acting in an incapable manner. Persons who exhibit fear or incompetence emit specific, hormone-related scents that tell a dog what their true feelings are; that's why scared people are more likely to be attacked by an aggressive dog than confident ones. Act as if you are scared or unsure and you risk losing his respect and obedience.

Watch your dog and home with the heightened senses of a canine, and the calm indifference of a true leader. Be aware without any trace of worry. Care, don't coddle!

Why Setting Boundaries Is Healthy and Safe

An essential role of any natural dog owner is to teach his or her dog what the physical and social boundaries of the "pack" are. Owners who fail at establishing what a dog can or cannot do or where he can or cannot go fail at a fundamental level to manage the dog/owner relationship.

Inadequate boundary training is an essential mistake of coddlers, who set no limits and expect nothing from a dog save a certain self-indulgent type of companionship. But a dog is not an animated Teddy bear; it is a purpose-driven mammal with a penchant for human company and a need for rules. If your sole motivation for getting a dog is to have a fuzzy foot warmer for cold nights, get a tabby!

Physical Boundaries

Physical boundaries include property lines, doors, windows, curbs, fences, or any delineation you decide applies to your dog. Even furniture; if you don't want your dog on the sofa or bed, make that an indisputable boundary issue. Same goes for areas in the home the dog is not welcome; if the baby's room or the bathroom are off-limits, then it's up to you to teach this to your pooch.

To teach boundaries, first teach your dog the "Wait" command (see Secret Two, Understand and Apply Leadership, the Sacred Canine Code). Designed to get a dog to momentarily wait at transitional spots such as doors, room entries or even rugs, "Wait" can be used to show your dog that certain borders cannot be crossed without consequences. If you want to teach him never to enter the baby's room, for instance, simply work the "Wait" at the entrance to the room, and just never give the "Okay" command to cross over the line. The "Wait" becomes in effect a permanent restriction.

Apply this principle to any boundary you set for your dog. Realize, however, that, if you are not present to enforce the rule, your dog will probably cross the imaginary boundary if he desires. So when not present, you should close doors and windows, or even install temporary impediments (such as a baby guard fence or baby-proof locks on all cupboards). These will ensure that your dog will never have access to a prohibited area.

I've found that if you physically prevent a dog from climbing up onto furniture for four or five months straight, the desire to climb up often subsides. So, if you want to keep your dog out of your easy chair while you are away, try placing a laundry basket atop it whenever you are gone, for four months straight. Most dogs will forget about the desire to use the chair, and won't even try it when the basket is removed. You can also use crumpled aluminum foil, or even the vacuum cleaner, which all dogs seem to despise.

Keeping your dog off the bed is as simple as keeping the door closed when you are away, and then simply correcting the dog if he climbs up in your presence. In fact, any room he isn't allowed to be in while you are gone should have a closeable door. Still work the "Wait" command, but use the door to reinforce the behavior while you are gone.

Boundaries apply to cars, too. While in the car, your dog needs to be in one secure spot without any chance of him interfering with your driving. Accidents occur when a dog interrupts a driver's actions, or else gets catapulted into the driver during an accident.

I usually keep my dogs in a travel crate in the back of my wagon; you can do this, or else secure him somewhere in the back of the car with a leash clipped to a dog harness and tied off on a headrest or part of a seat mounting. *Never* restrain your dog in the car by means of a leash clipped to his collar, as he could be strangled in an accident.

An option is to purchase a dog restraint harness system, designed to work along with a rear seatbelt. Available at most pet stores, they do a great job of securing your dog and keeping him safe. In my opinion, safety harnesses and travel crates are the best ways to maintain boundaries and keep both you and your dog perfectly safe during a road trip.

Psychological Boundaries

Treated as seriously as physical borders, psychological boundaries are necessary to teach manners and respect, and to reinforce the pecking order.

Jumping up on people should be prohibited, especially with children or the elderly. It's rude and shouldn't be allowed, period. Dogs that jump up are usually poorly trained coddler pets with little leadership coming from the top. Don't let your dog cross this annoying line!

Stealing food from other pets is another boundary no-no. Even if a dog is clearly dominant over another pet, food is an essential right, and should be respected as such. Toys, beds or other "possessions" can be argued over, but never food.

Growling at or biting any human is a huge psychological boundary gaffe; if your dog does this, even with kids or strangers, it means that he has major socialization or leadership issues, and could be either profoundly fear aggressive or simply a dominant cuss. It may mean that you have not established yourself as the leader, causing him to fret over interactions, or think that he is the boss, and has the right to discipline anyone he chooses. Either way, you have a problem.

To deal with this, reread Secret Two, and apply all you learn to your dog. Sharpen your dog's obedience, and brook no exceptions to the idea that humans are above him in the pack. If your dog shows lasting, profound aggression, get help from a trained dog behaviorist to diagnose and treat the problem.

An exception to this perspective is if someone tries to maliciously attack you or your dog, or break into your home. Then all bets are off; even the best of dogs should defend you and the home territory. If it's three o'clock in the morning and guys with masks are sneaking around your living room, let your dog rock!

Physical and psychological boundaries help your dog discern right from wrong, and teach him proper pack etiquette. Be sure to teach him where curiosity and free expression end, and where courtesy and respect begin!

Endow Your Dog with Purpose

The Purpose-Driven Dog

We expand the idea of life purpose to include the abstractions of philosophy, art, politics and religion. But dogs have no such constructs; they simply want to do what dogs do best, as often as possible. Their pragmatic, goal-driven nature remains as true today as it did ten thousand years past. As a natural dog owner, you should honor that spirit.

The wolf pack's purpose is to hunt, raise healthy pups to maturity, and support the safety and solidarity of the group. Though similar in intent, domestic dogs have more narrowly defined drives than wolves, as defined by breed-type. As discussed in Secret One, breed-specific traits determine not only how a dog looks, but also how he acts; this behavioral specialization helps determine what a particular dog's purpose should be.

If you were a Bloodhound, what would your heart-felt purpose in life be? Right: *follow the scent for as long as it takes.* In fact, working bloodhounds have been known to stay on the scent of lost persons or escaped prisoners for over fifty miles! Now, if you were instead a Pug, would you have the same purpose? Hardly, as this happy breed has below-average scent abilities, and is better suited to serving as a companion dog.

For every dog there is a special purpose, arrived at through breed, personality and experience. My old dog Louie, a Rottweiler mix, loved to perform tricks, help teach other dogs, and explore the woods. My Shepherd mix Flavio loves to fetch and run; Johnny, a Cairn terrier mix I once owned, lived to chase squirrels and tennis balls. The point is all dogs crave a muse or goal.

Neither dog nor owner can long maintain good spirits without having some special purpose to aspire to. Knowing this, natural owners set goals and challenges for their dogs. By doing so, their dogs wake each morning with desire and motivation. Secret Seven teaches readers the vital importance of purpose, and shows how to challenge their dogs' innate desire to perform and succeed.

This doesn't mean you should hyper-focus on or spoil your dog; really the opposite is true. In fact, giving your dog a purpose-driven activity is the most "canine" thing you can do. It's true empathy at work when an owner treats a dog less like a nursery school child and more like a pack member yearning for doggish pursuits.

Identifying Your Dog's Purpose

As mentioned, a combination of breed, personality and experience determines what your dog really likes to do. If you have an active sporting breed or breed mix, for example, odds are he has lots of energy and a drive to stalk, retrieve or swim. Because he has been bred to work closely with humans, he will have a cooperative nature, and a desire to work for attention and praise. Combining these qualities with an amiable personality and a fondness for physical activity gives you a dog that should love outdoor pursuits, or anything that involves fetching, running, retrieving, or complex agility or obedience work.

What if your dog isn't as personable or willing? Say you own a Basenji, a breed known to be active, discerning, and a bit stubborn? An ancient African hunting breed, the lithe, alert Basenji is still used there to drive small game into nets. As with all sighthounds, they can run like the wind. The breed's independent mindset often makes them hard to train; without regular, purpose-driven activity, they can get cabin fever and become real home wreckers.

What do some Basenji owners do to direct their breeds' energies? An organized activity known as *lure coursing*, in which sighthounds chase a fast-moving lure (usually a bright plastic bag towed by a motorcycle) around a course, and are judged according to speed, agility, enthusiasm and ability to follow. Extremely popular with sighthound owners, lure coursing taps the Basenji's innate desire to chase and capture small game. If you own a Basenji (or another sighthound breed-type) with an independent streak and plenty of prey drive, this would be a great venue for him to express purpose. At the very least, you could set up your own lure course, with a friend or child on a bicycle pulling a tempting lure on the end of a long rope.

Of course every dog will show individual likes or dislikes; it's up to you to pay attention and discern what these are, and then select a purpose-driven activity best suited to match his unique needs. Determine what he loves best, then direct that instinct into one or more of the suggestions that follow.

Breed Group Tendencies

Each breed group has a unique behavioral "fingerprint." Knowing this will help you select activities for your dog to participate in. Let's look at how the groups differ:

Sporting Active, outgoing and friendly, Sporting group dogs excel at energetic activities involving close cooperation with humans. Retrievers, pointers and spaniels dominate the group; they love to perform tricks and obedience behaviors and "Fetch," love to swim and stalk, and excel at agility. The operative idea here is athletic teamwork; they live to please!

Hounds Separated into two subgroups, all hounds show an independent mindset and intense focus on the job at hand. Unlike dogs in the sporting group, hounds often work without the close interaction of an owner, and as such can show a somewhat stubborn, independent streak. Scenthounds like the Beagle or Bloodhound use their incredible noses to track down persons or objects, while sighthounds like the Greyhound or Saluki use keen vision and explosive speed to locate and capture small game or moving lures. Scenthounds excel at tracking activities, while sighthounds love to race or chase after simulated prey.

Working Bred to protect, pull loads or rescue people, dogs in the working group are strong, smart, and self-sufficient. The Siberian Husky, Rottweiler and others tend toward the large side, and require a competent owner to direct their power, loyalty and individuality. Choose an activity that challenges their strength, courage and intelligence. Working dogs love to perform obedience behaviors, guard the home territory, swim, pull heavy loads, and play active outdoor games such as hide-and-seek or tag. Just about any activity involving strength and stamina will work well.

Terriers Known for their tenacity, terriers were bred to hunt vermin. Competitive and independent-minded, these small to medium-sized dogs think they are larger than they really are. Owners of terriers such as the Cairn, Irish, Norwich and others need determination and consistency when training, and should choose purpose-driven activities that sate the terrier's need to stalk prey. Stalk-and-capture games like "Fetch" work well, as do controlled games of "Find-it," where the item is animated and hidden. They also do well in agility and obedience if properly trained.

Toys A group categorized by their diminutive size, dogs in the toy group were bred as companion pets, and as such have a penchant for human camaraderie. Don't let their small size fool you; they can be just as feisty and active as the other breed groups. Though toys like the Maltese and English Toy Spaniel tend toward the placid side, others like the Chihuahua, Miniature Pinscher or Toy Fox Terrier can be little balls of fire. Purpose-driven activities depends on the breed's roots; a toy spaniel for instance will have similar stalking/flushing drives to his larger spaniel counterparts, while a Yorkshire terrier will act like a terrier. Smart, sociable toys like the Maltese, Chinese Crested or Teacup Poodle may enjoy learning tricks, as it requires close positive contact with humans.

Non-Sporting Like the Toy and Miscellaneous groups, the Non-Sporting group is a collection of somewhat unrelated breeds that don't quite fit into any of the other better-defined collections. For instance; the Poodle, originally a hunting breed, is located in this group, as is the Chow Chow, an ancient guarding breed that couldn't be more different from a Poodle in temperament and drive. A Poodle will love to "Fetch," swim, or perform tricks; a Chow Chow will love scaring off the solicitors! The lively Boston Terrier, with a friendly, near toy-like demeanor, couldn't be more different than the Dalmatian, a breed with hunting roots and an extraordinary affinity for horses. Take a Boston to agility class; bring your Dalmatian to a horse farm!

If you own a breed in this group, do your breed research and choose an activity best suited to your dog's heritage. Don't forget individual personality either; if your Chow Chow likes to "Fetch," go for it!

Herding Here is a group of independent whiz kids. Bred to control large, fast-moving farm animals, breeds like the Border Collie and Corgi live to manage the position of animals and humans alike. By all means, if you can find a herding club close by, give it a try. If not, realize that these highly intelligent, driven breeds can excel at competitive obedience, agility competition, flyball, trick training, or just about any activity requiring speed and intellect.

Miscellaneous Another grouping of unrelated breeds, the Miscellaneous group acts as a "probationary" holding area, where certain breeds wait for official recognition and assignment to an appropriate group. For instance, the Beauceron and Swedish Vallhund, two herding-type breeds, will most likely be reassigned to the Herding group by the time this book goes to press. The Redbone Coonhound is also here; a true scenthound, it will eventually be relocated to the Hound group. Again, if you own a breed in this group, do your research, and choose accordingly.

Mixed Breeds

As stated in Secret One, if you own a mixed-breed dog, you probably have a good idea what breeds constitute his lineage. Once you determine this to the best of your ability, you need only select purpose-driven activities best suited to that mix. For instance, a Shepherd/Retriever mix will be a smart dog with a penchant for fetching, tracking and herding. A Terrier/Poodle mix will be a smart, feisty dog with an aptitude for tricks, agility and retrieving. A Dalmatian/Greyhound mix will be reserved and fast; consider jogging or swimming. And don't forget to factor in your mixed breed's personality and previous experience; if he likes to search out moles in the backyard, take him to a tracking class!

Purpose-driven Activities

A huge range of purpose-driven activities exists for you to choose from; it's up to you to decide upon one or more, according to your dog's tendencies and passions. Let's look at some:

Retrieving

Any dog with retriever, spaniel, pointer or setter breed heritage will love to retrieve a ball over and over. It is their original purpose, and most still heartily ascribe to it. Other breeds (such as the herders) will also retrieve, though some dogs (such as the Arctic breeds or scenthounds) may not be as adept at actually bringing the ball back to you.

For dogs that enjoy it, retrieving can be the most heart-felt, enjoyable activity going. Teach "Fetch" according to the directions in Secret Four, under the "*Give*" subheading.

Competitive Obedience

Canine clubs and organizations the world over sponsor and support competitive obedience trials for both purebred and mixed-breed dogs. As with any sport, competition sharpens and improves the ability to perform; this applies especially to dogs, that seem to thrive in competitive surroundings. As purpose-driven activities go, competitive obedience rates right near the top.

With competition comes heightened aptitude, and the ability to perform complex linked behaviors with great distraction. Granted, it's not for all dogs; but for natural owners with trainable, eager canine students, competing for obedience titles can bring out the best in a dog.

Obedience competitions are usually broken down into three levels of increasing competence: *Novice*, *Open*, and *Utility*. All are judged by impartial judges. Here is a quick summary of what each level expects of you and your dog:

Novice The beginner's level, Novice first requires you and your dog to perform an on-leash "Heel," with an automatic "Sit" whenever you stop. During the exercise, you are asked to halt, change direction and pace, and perform a smooth figure-eight around two posts.

Next is a standing exam, performed by the judge with you standing six feet off. The judge touches your dog's head, back and rear, during which time the pet must not break position.

The "Heel" is again performed, only off leash. With many other people and dogs present, this can be a challenge to even the most eager dogs.

Then your dog must perform a perfect recall, or "Come Here." You "Heel" your dog out to a spot and have him "Sit," then you walk to the opposite side of the ring. When the judge signals you, you call your dog to you; he must come the very first time, sit in front of you, then circle around you to your left side and sit in a proper "Heel" position.

After this your dog must successfully complete a group "Sit-Stay" and a group "Down-Stay." Then it's over! Sound easy?

Each dog begins the trial with 200 points, with the judge deducting for errors during the event. Any dog with at least 170 points remaining wins a "leg" toward the title. Win three legs and your dog gets the Companion Dog title, or "CD."

Open Now it gets harder (if you can believe it). All exercises for the Open level are done *off leash*. First is a "Heel" with changes in pace and direction, and the same figure-eight pattern.

Then a recall is performed, during which your dog must instantly drop down into a "Down" on command when about halfway back. This takes great focus and control on the dog's behalf.

Your dog's ability to retrieve an object is then tested. He must bring back the item across a flat route, and then over a high jump. If you have a retriever, it should be easy; if you have a Husky or Chihuahua, good luck!

After the retrieve, your pooch must perform a broad jump. Then, once group "Sit-Stays" and "Down-Stays" are successfully completed, your dog is done. If he scores 170 points or more, he earns one leg toward his Companion Dog Excellent title, or "CDX." Two more legs and he gets it!

Utility Few dogs ever get their Utility Dog or "UD" title. Those that do are special dogs of uncanny intelligence and ability, with highly skilled owners. I'll lay out the requirements for you in case you have the motivation and time to get this far. Mind you—it takes years to get a dog to this level of ability.

After a complex off-leash "Heel" is performed (using hand signals only), your dog goes through a meticulous physical exam by the judge. Then "Sit," "Down," "Come Here" and "Return to Heel" are all performed, again with hand signals only.

Now comes the hard stuff. Your dog must now correctly pick two objects, handled only by you, out of a pile of similar objects, using only your scent as his guide. Then a "directed retrieve" is done; of three gloves laid out on the floor, your dog must retrieve the one you direct him to retrieve.

Last is the high jump and bar jump. Once completed, your dog gets one leg of three if at least 170 points remain. Two more legs and he gets his Utility Dog, or "UD" title. Simple, right?

Few owners have the time or skill to reach this level. Don't let that stop you though; even getting through the first leg of Novice will be a great achievement for you both, and a perfect way to add purpose to your dog's world.

Agility Competition

A growing sport in which dogs must correctly and quickly navigate a series of obstacles under the guidance of their handlers, agility competition is a fun activity for all, and a marvelous purpose-driven pursuit. The obstacles include jumps, tunnels, a seesaw, narrow elevated walking platforms, an "A" frame walkover, weave poles, and a table upon which the dog must sit or lie down for a specified length of time. Owner/handlers run with their dogs and guide them to the correct obstacle with verbal commands and hand signals.

In the United States and Europe, major agility organizations hold trials where dog/handler teams compete. Complexity of the course increases in difficulty as a dog progresses through three levels of competition—from starters/novice through open/advanced and into the masters/elite/excellent classes.

The sense of enjoyment and teamwork developed from training a dog in agility can't help but deepen your connection with your dog. If you are interested in giving it a try, check with local dog training facilities for a referral to a local agility club, or do a web search on the subject. I guarantee there is an agility club close by.

Disk Competition

Soon after the invention of the flying disk toy, dog owners began using them to have fun with their dogs. Nothing is quite as enjoyable as lofting one up and having your dog leap up like a gazelle to catch it in midair.

Today, flying disk competitions sponsored the world over attract thousands of people and their dogs. The premise of disk competition is simple: score as many points as possible in sixty seconds by having your dog catch flying disks in mid-air. Scoring basically depends upon the distance a disk has traveled before being caught by the dog.

Dogs that compete in disk competitions are capable of great athleticism. Border Collies, Whippets, Jack Russell terriers, Australian Shepherds and other agile, energetic breed-types all do well, as do any dogs with adequate physical strength and speed. As purpose-driven activities go, this one rates high for dogs with that extra "get up and go."

If your dog loves to catch, fetch and jump, think about contacting a local flying disk club and enrolling in classes. Like agility classes, the experience will add purpose to your dog's world, and strengthen the bond between you.

Tracking

Years ago a training facility I worked at received a call from a local winery; they wanted to discuss a pressing issue, but wouldn't go any further on the phone. Intrigued, we visited the winery and had a fascinating meeting.

A type of cork fungus was tainting their wine and rendering it undrinkable. As a result, the wine industry was losing millions of dollars each year on returned product. Problem was, the fungus was invisible, and odorless (at least to humans). They wanted to know if we could train dogs to detect the fungus before the wine was bottled!

We of course said yes. After obtaining from them a pure sample of the fungus, we began scent-training six shelter dogs for the job. The dogs ranged from a Jack Russell terrier to a German Shepherd to an Irish Setter mix; all were high-energy dogs that had shown great play/retrieve drives, and high aptitudes for scent work.

It took several months, but we did it. Essentially we first got each dog excited about a particular toy, and then played "find-it" games with them. Once each became enamored of a specific toy, we began "inoculating" it with a sample of the fungus.

Eventually each dog began to subconsciously associate the toy with the fungal smell; they would soon begin "finding" their respective toys by tracking them down with their noses. In this way, we taught them to play "find the fungus."

We then took them to the winery for a test. Fifty huge bales of corks were lined up waiting for us, each containing thousands of corks; only *one* tainted cork in *one* bale actually had the fungus; the rest were fine.

We had devised "tell" signs for the dogs, a specific signaling behavior that would alert us to when the dog smelled the fungus. Some barked, while others sat or lay down. After having each dog run atop the bales a few times, sniffing along the way, we found that each would invariably stop on the *same* bale and give us the signal, whereupon we would reward him with his special toy. To prevent one dog from mimicking another's behavior, we made sure to keep the others out of the room while running a specific dog.

They each detected one tainted cork out of a million! The wine executives were amazed, as were we. For the next two years, we made weekly trips to the winery to test bales of corks for the fungus. In two years we compiled a 97 percent accuracy rating, saving the winery millions.

The winery ultimately came up with a cheaper chemical test for the fungus, putting our woolly sniffers out of business. But, in the meantime, we had shown what six shelter mutts could do with a little training and a lot of enthusiasm.

Where we have at best a myopic sense of smell, dogs have olfactory "radar," a sense so sharp that they can actually follow a faint scent trail and locate a person or object, sometimes from miles off. Police and military canine units take advantage of this every day, as do hunters and civilian rescue organizations. Some dogs have even been trained to detect cancer cells, or looming epileptic seizures!

You can train your dog to track a person or find an object through scent. Though not easy, many local tracking clubs exist that are willing to take on new members, and teach the fine art of tracking to eager students. A great purpose-driven activity, it is usually done outdoors in large fields, with the dogs tethered on long leads and trained to follow scent trails. The activity is a fun way to get your dog in touch with his greatest asset, his nose.

To learn more, contact any local dog training school and ask about tracking classes in your area. Or, do a web search for local tracking clubs. Try also contacting national dog clubs and asking about tracking clubs in your area. Whatever level you decide to take it to, working scent-tracking activities will increase your respect for your dog, and help you to become the natural owner you want to be.

To get a feel for how sharp your dog's nose is, hide a few aromatic treats around the home or yard, as discussed in Secret Five: Enrich Your

Dog's Environment. Most dogs will quickly sense the presence of
the goodies, and start searching in earnest. Breeds like the Beagle,
Dachshund, German Shepherd Dog and Bassett Hound will be particularly excited by this, as their noses are among the most keen. If you pass
on tracking classes, consider using this simpler purpose-driven activity
on a regular basis.

Flyball

An incredibly fun experience, "Flyball" is a popular, organized activity
whose goal is to test how fast four-dog teams can run a relay race. The
course has four hurdles spaced ten feet apart, and a spring-loaded box at
the end of the run that ejects a tennis ball when stepped on by the dog.
Each dog must jump over the hurdles, step on the box, catch the ejected
tennis ball, then run back over the hurdles and cross a finish line. The
next dog on the team then repeats the same procedure; the first team to
finish the course without mistakes wins the heat. When properly done,
it's exciting to watch.

Flyball's complexity tests a dog's agility, speed, dexterity, sociability,
and competitive drive. It's fun for all, and, like tracking, perfect for
owners who want to go beyond teaching simplistic obedience behavior
or tricks.

Most dogs competing in Flyball have great intelligence and a desire
to run. In fact, it's no accident that so many of them come from
herding stock. If your dog shows a high drive for retrieving, herding
and running, consider contacting a Flyball club in your area and
attending a tournament, to see if you and your dog might be interested.
To find a club near you, contact a local training facility for information,
or check online.

Hunting

Every dog on the planet is a hunter by nature. Once a primary function
for many dogs, the "job" of hunting has become but a novelty, limited
mostly to bird dogs used by recreational hunters.

Today, most of us do our hunting down the aisles of the local supermarket. A disconnect between the neatly packaged portions of meat we purchase and the actual animal has developed, insulating us from the reality of the kill. No such rationalization exists for your dog, who may find our inability to personally slay our own dinners confusing, if not downright humorous.

Though I do not hunt, I see nothing wrong with the practice provided the meat is used for practical purposes. To that end, those who wish to hunt with their dogs will find it to be one of the most complete purpose-driven activities going. After all, it's what nature designed dogs to do best.

The most common use for dogs in hunting today is as gun dogs that locate and reveal the presence of differing species of game birds, and in some cases flush them into the air to give the hunter a clean shot. Retrievers excel at finding and retrieving shot fowl from the water; their "soft" mouths ensure that prey will be returned to the hunter in one piece. Pointers and Setters are bred to locate coveys of grounded birds, then freeze in a classic pointing or "setting" position, until the hunter can get into position. Then the dog flushes the prey into the air, allowing the hunter a clean shot. Spaniels do similar work, but can do so from thicker, closer brush, due to their smaller size. Water dogs such as Poodles and Irish Water Spaniels hunt in a fashion similar to the Retrievers, and are in fact the oldest of bird dog breeds.

Dogs are sometimes used to track, flush and tree large game such as bear, cougar, fox and wolf. I don't condone this, unless the animal in question has killed or wounded a human being and needs to be tracked down and killed. When large packs of dogs are used to tree a cougar or bear until a hunter can come and dispatch the animal, the element of "sport" becomes in my opinion dubious at best. I am not against hunting per say, but simply against the removal of any chance of the hunted actually evading the hunter. After all, shouldn't the thrill of hunting include the chance of the prey getting away? Using five or six dogs to corral an animal up a tree doesn't sound very sporting to me.

If you are an avid bird hunter, using your Retriever, Pointer, Setter, Spaniel or other hunting breed will tap his need for purpose like no other activity. However, the activity requires that your dog be trained from puppyhood to perform this complex task; if your dog is older than four or five months, it's probably too late to start. You could of course purchase a new puppy and start the training early on.

If you are interested in becoming involved in the sport, I recommend you first go out with a veteran hunter to fully appreciate the experience. If still interested, join a local bird-hunting club, and take the proper gun safety classes!

Herding

Anyone who owns a herding breed knows how driven these dogs are. Kids, cars, bikes, pets—whatever moves, the herder wants to herd them, control them, covet them.

Like the herding dogs used by the Basques, today's Border Collies, Australian Shepherds, Corgis and others want to put their instincts to good use. When unable to do so, these athletic control freaks tend to go stir-crazy. Perhaps more than any other group of dogs, herders need purpose-driven activities on a regular basis.

If you have a hardy dog capable of running for long periods of time, consider locating a sheep-herding club in your area. Usually located in suburban or rural areas, these clubs will help you teach your dog to run with the sheep, just as the Basques did with their dogs. Though herding breed-types naturally excel at this, most dogs will catch on, or at least give it a try. If you have a Border Collie, Australian Shepherd, or other traditional herder, this is almost a prerequisite for you! Small dogs do run the risk of getting injured by the sheep, so pass on herding if you own a dog under thirty pounds, unless you can find a club that uses ducks for small dogs. Also, dogs with extremely high prey or territorial drives often make poor herding dogs, as they might injure the sheep. The herding club director will help you decide if your dog is a good candidate for this excellent enrichment activity.

Club personnel will first give your dog a preliminary test to determine his ability to move and control livestock (sheep, cattle or ducks); if he passes he'll be given the chance to learn basic skills, while you learn basic handler expertise. If you both excel, competitive, judged events follow.

Herding is time-consuming and dependent upon the availability of space and livestock; those living in the city might find the long trips into the country a bit taxing. But if you can find a local herding venue and a club willing to train you, it will be well worth it. You'll see a side of your dog you never thought possible!

Guarding

One of my basic rules regarding leadership is that you, the leader, must be in charge of protecting the pack. It's just not your dog's job to initiate interactions, be they friendly or otherwise. That said, when a real threat to the pack occurs, all members must cooperate together to defend life and property.

All dogs, no matter how submissive or dominant, desire to protect the pack. It is a natural instinct that's hard to turn off. Even the most loving Lab will bark and growl at a bang on your door at three in the morning. As long as you do not encourage or magnify this instinct, it's a *good* thing, and a way for your dog to express purpose.

I'm not at all in favor of encouraging your dog to attack or display aggression toward strangers or strange animals. That happens all too often with foolish owners whose own false bravado leads to unnecessary dog aggression. It has stained the reputations of several breeds, including pit bulls, Rottweiler and others. What I am suggesting is that you do allow your dog to respond instinctively to any unprovoked, dangerous assault upon himself, you, your family, or your home. For instance, if an aggressive stray dog were to bolt up to you during a walk and so threaten you or your dog, it is totally acceptable *and desirable* for your dog to protect you, provided you do all you can to do the same. Or, if you are fast asleep and an intruder attempts entry into your home, it's your dog's *duty* to bark, alerting you to the threat.

So, how can one allow a dog to express this innate, purpose-driven guarding activity without encouraging unnecessary aggression? With regard to the home, if your dog has been properly socialized and trained, he will know the difference between an acceptable visit and a late-night invasion. His senses and instincts will engage; he will know that no one acceptable comes crashing in at 3 a.m. This unusual "visit" will inspire him to bark. That's good! At that point, you'll wake up and evaluate the situation. If it's a friend, you can calm the dog down and deal with the situation, but if it's a burglar, all bets are off; you and your dog have the duty to get down.

Regarding assaults upon you or your dog while out and about, it's up to you to determine the threat level. If at all possible, deal with the situation yourself in a calm manner. This will keep your own dog calm and avoid conditioning him into reacting in a defensive manner whenever strangers approach. But if you feel your life is threatened, your own visceral reaction will tell your dog what to do. He'll sense your legitimate fear and react to your defensive posturing. At this point, he will become part of a team, dedicated to protecting the pack. The *sheer rarity* of fear expressed by you, a natural leader, will inspire him to action.

Consider allowing your dog to be loose in the home while you sleep. This will allow him to use his superior senses to detect anything out of the ordinary, including not only an intruder, but fire, a gas leak or flood, or even a sick or injured child. Dogs save the lives of their owners every day in exactly this manner; give your dog the chance to do it, too, and you'll be honoring his most purposeful instincts.

Challenge Him!

Apart from finding a specific, purpose-driven activity for your dog to participate in, you should strive to generalize the idea of purpose, and make even everyday activities challenging and stimulating. For instance, if while walking him you notice that he likes to chase blowing leaves, let him! He'll have fun exercising his latent stalking drive. And from this you will learn that he needs a bit more stimulation in that area; to have him express it, teach him to fetch a ball or flying disk. You could even create a game in which he chases windblown leaves or even paper airplanes around the yard, in exchange for a reward.

Make mundane events more exciting. For instance, when letting him outside just before bedtime, let him relieve himself first, then run out there like a nutcase to play a quick game of tag. Do this randomly, so he never knows when it will happen. This will jazz him up and make the last memory of the day more exciting.

Even walks or romps in the park can take on purpose. Don't let this time spent together become monotonous or rote; instead, let them become adventures during which time the "pack" explores, searches, stalks and plays. *Be the dog*; let him see you chase a squirrel up a tree, catch a friend's flying disk, jump in the lake, or bark at a crow! Set a confident, doggish example for him, and always keep it interesting. And be sure to allow him to express his own personality, provided it doesn't conflict with your leadership or his need for manners.

Lastly, pay attention to what your dog loves, and to what he has a real aptitude for. Then invent purpose-driven activities that reflect these likes and abilities. Through it all, be sure he earns your respect and attention; remember: *educate, don't placate!*

Conclusion

Honor the Bond

In history, have two species been more enamored of each other than dogs and humans? Together we have searched for challenge, good times and acceptance. We have shared ravenous appetite, and loathed failure or anonymity; among all other animals, are there two more willing and able to look each other straight in the eye?

What other creatures share such a bond? Cattle and their egrets? Sharks and their remoras? No, the dog/human link is inspirational, so much so that some deny the link and chose instead to see their dogs as doppelgangers, instead of a part of nature breaking through the wild mystery to call us friend.

Above all, this book has attempted to show how unique dogs are, and how in honoring this uniqueness we make the dog/owner relationship more meaningful. Treat a dog like a coddled toddler and you get a troubled pariah; connect with him on his own level and you discover what being a dog really means.

My goal is to convince owners to treat their dogs *like dogs,* not people. Doing so will remove a great weight from about their dogs' necks, and allow owners to experience their pets from a wholly new, natural perspective.

Summary of the Seven Secrets

Abiding by the Seven Secrets is the best way to experience what your dog is all about. Let's revisit them one more time:

Choose Your Friends Wisely

Dogs are like automobiles, some big as ponies, others small as purses. Many have boundless energy, while others take the time to sniff the roses. Dogs can be social butterflies or shrinking violets; truly, their physical and behavioral diversity is nearly limitless.

Choose a dog that matches your lifestyle, space, and personal preference. Don't get a Formula One racer if you haven't got the track! Kids? Choose a dog that loves endless physical attention. Jogger? Choose an aerobic powerhouse. Big person with a booming voice and commanding presence? Pick a strong, extroverted dog that will revel in your charisma. Match the dog to the conditions, and to your own capabilities and expectations.

For the majority of readers who already have a dog, learn as much as you can about its breed heritage and personal history, to create the best dog/owner interface, and to best fine-tune the home environment to the pet's true nature. Give the dog what it needs to express its natural inclinations!

Understand and Apply Leadership, the Sacred Canine Code

Remember: dogs don't vote. Instead, they prefer an age-old construct known as the leadership hierarchy, with an alpha leader atop the pack directing, disciplining and protecting. Dogs feel calm and contented when their owners run the show, and nervous and adrift when owners give parity. Coddle your dog and problems abound; lead your dog and it all falls into place.

Embrace a Canine Attitude and Awareness

Never try to turn your dog into a proxy human; instead turn yourself into a proxy dog. Embrace what I call *effective canine empathy*, which demands you see things from a dog's perspective. Be the dog! Once you begin to see things from a dog's eye view, you'll better appreciate the canine condition, and understand why your dog does the things he does. This special inter-species empathy is crucial to becoming a natural dog owner. He can't do it, but you can.

Turbocharge Your Dog's IQ

The more you teach your dog, the smarter he will get. And a smart, edu-cated dog is more thoughtful, calmer and better prepared for life than a dog with little training or aptitude. Dogs with large vocabularies and diverse behavioral choices tend to be friendlier and more adaptable than dogs isolated from learning. To create a smarter, calmer, better-adjusted dog, teach him!

Enrich Your Dog's Environment

Most dogs live in stimulus-poor surroundings. With little to do or experi-ence, they become bored little troublemakers. You can change this by turning your dog's environment into a more interesting place. Hidden treat trails, olfactory enticements, relocation of food dishes, trips to the dog park, doggy day cares—whatever it takes to stimulate his mind and body, and engage his imagination.

Keep Your Dog Healthy and Safe

As your dog's natural leader, you are in charge of keeping him safe and healthy. This means feeding him an optimal diet to encourage good health and avoid obesity, providing exercise to strengthen the body and release stress, and visiting the veterinarian regularly to prevent illness or disease. It also means dog-proofing the home to prevent accidents, and defending your dog if and when the need arises. Remember that you are the captain; the well-being of your crew is in your hands. A secure, healthy dog is always happier and better behaved than one that feels sickly and scared.

Endow Your Dog with Purpose

Dogs are purpose-driven animals in need of a constant muse. Unaware of this, many owners fail to provide their pets with opportunities to express their innate canine "programming." Unable to stalk, retrieve, herd, track or guard, dogs become depressed and stressed, leading to misbehavior. As a natural owner, you should set goals and challenges for your dog based upon his breed-specific tendencies and personal preferences. Doing so stokes his desire and motivation, and appeals to his desire to perform and succeed.

Your Dog as a Role Model

After following the Seven Secrets for a time, your dog will morph into a calmer, more enjoyable pet. He'll be a happier dog, and a better friend to you. You will change too, from a person who simply loves and admires dogs to someone who speaks their language. And you will begin to see how well *effective canine empathy* works to improve not only your own dog, but others too.

Dogs benefiting from the Seven-Secret lifestyle become superb role models for other dogs and their owners. When your friends see how calm, well behaved and integrated your dog is, they will want to know your "secret." Show them by example; let them spend time with you and your dog, to see how effective and rewarding the lifestyle is. In due course they will abandon the ways of the "Coddler" in favor of the ways of the "Natural," and their dogs will become dogs again. Hopefully part of them will, too.

I'd like to one day see the fad of humanizing and coddling dogs peak and fade. Nothing would be more successful at reducing behavioral problems and restoring the natural balance between us. This book is a beginning; perhaps by winning you and your dogs over I'll start a new trend, one which respects dogs for who and what they are, instead of one attempting to recreate them in our own image. By embracing effective *canine empathy* and becoming a caring, competent leader to your dog, you can make a difference, and set an example for others. Remember:

BE THE DOG!

Index

About the Author

Pet behaviorist and native New Yorker **Steve Duno** has trained thousands of animals. His fifteen books and innumerable Web and magazine articles have covered a wide variety of topics including breed profiling, obedience training, pet diet and health care, solutions for aggression and other problem behaviors, and even trick training for both dogs and cats. A former teacher, Steve has also written fiction, and even two golf books (in his spare time). His books have garnered him appearances on television and radio.

Steve Dunno lives in Seattle with his family, his ditsy shepard mix Flavio, and his über mutt Rico.